How to Get Your Children to What You Want Them to Do

How to Get Your Children to Do What You Want Them to Do

by
Paul Wood, M.D.
and
Bernard Schwartz

PRENTICE-HALL, INC., Englewood Cliffs, N.J.

How to Get Your Children to Do What You Want Them to Do
by Paul Wood, M.D.
and Bernard Schwartz

Copyright © 1977 by Paul Wood
and Bernard Schwartz
Printed in the United States of America
Prentice-Hall International, Inc., London
Prentice-Hall of Australia, Pty. Ltd., Sydney
Prentice-Hall of Canada, Ltd., Toronto
Prentice-Hall of India Private Ltd., New Delhi
Prentice-Hall of Japan, Inc., Tokyo
Prentice-Hall of Southeast Asia Pte. Ltd., Singapore
Whitehall Books Limited, Wellington, New Zealand

10 9

Library of Congress Cataloging in Publication Data
Wood, Paul,
    How to get your children to do what you want
them to do.
    Bibliography: p.
    1. Children—Management.   2. Discipline of
children.   3. Interpersonal communication.
I. Schwartz, Bernard, joint author.   II. Title.
HQ772.W6 1977   649'.1   76-54846
ISBN 0 13-409797-1
ISBN-0-13-409821-8 pbk.

TO OUR
PARENTS
AND FAMILIES

ACKNOWLEDGMENTS

The concepts presented in this book represent a departure from the traditional methods of dealing with behavior problems in children. The authors are especially indebted to Randall M. Foster, M.D., for introducing these concepts to us and for teaching us that parents are capable of getting their children to do what they want them to do.

We also wish to express our appreciation to our students, patients, and colleagues from whom we have gained much insight and knowledge.

We also lovingly thank Karen and Jan for their patience and continual support and encouragement throughout this project.

INTRODUCTION

"Scooter" is five years old. He has gotten into trouble at school numerous times for kicking and hitting other children. His parents complain that at home he gets into everything from his dad's tools to his mother's cosmetics.

Andrea is seven. She has trouble getting along with her brother and sister and is also still wetting the bed. Her parents are concerned because nothing they do seems to please her.

Janet is fourteen. She has cut classes often this semester and has run away from home on several occasions. She is now involved with the juvenile authorities as a result of being caught with an assortment of drugs in her possession.

Gerald is fifteen. He often stays out later than his parents would like him to. He's falling behind in his schoolwork, and his parents complain that they've tried everything to get him to do his household chores, but nothing works.

These are a sample of the many types of problems which parents experience in raising their children.

How to Get Your Children to Do What You Want Them to Do helps parents to understand the cause of these and other behavioral or emotional problems, and then explains step-by-step how to correct and prevent these difficulties.

This is a relatively short book for two reasons.

One is that to prevent or correct problem behaviors is just not as complicated as it has been made out to be. Certainly it is not an easy task. But the difficulty is not in understanding *how to do it*. Whatever difficulty there is lies in the time, energy, and patience required to put these concepts into practice.

Can there really be anything new under the sun with regard to this subject, considering the overwhelming number of books already available? Without hesitation we can answer this question with an emphatic yes.

Though much of what has been written is valuable, a few key points in understanding and correcting behavioral problems have been totally missed. It seems to be a case of not being able to see the forest for the trees. In the course of analyzing parental difficulties, we have too often lost the total picture. This we have found to be true of psychoanalytically-oriented books which often help parents understand their child, but still not know how to deal with him; and with behavior modification type books which frequently leave parents frustrated in their efforts to find a suitable reward or punishment with which to change their child's behavior. The reason for our unabashed belief in the principles presented in this book is the authors' dramatically successful clinical experiences with thousands of children, as well as the reports of teachers, probation officers, social workers, and other therapists who have found this approach equally effective. In addition, many of the children we have seen had previously been through long-term, costly approaches to family problems to no avail, yet responded within one or two sessions when their parents applied the concepts which are described in this book. The explanation for the effectiveness of this approach lies in its ability to be used regardless of the type of problem or age of the child.

The second reason for the brevity of this book is that it is by no means a total or comprehensive child-rearing book. It focuses specifically on the "how's and why's" of problem behaviors. There is certainly more to the parent-child relationship than getting children to do what you want them to do. However, the premise of this book is that before parents can develop this relationship to its highest level, fundamental issues must be dealt with first The prevention and correction of ongoing misbehaviors is, we feel, the most fundamental issue. To do this entails establishing a clear-cut parent-child relationship. That is, it must be clear who is in the leadership role. Until that is well defined, it will not help to read an entire library of books on child psychology and development. This book shows parents how to define that relationship so that they can get on with the other, more pleasurable parts of parenthood: nurturing the child, enjoying the child, and watching the child grow and succeed in life.

Another factor which distinguishes this book from others is that the approach we present is a positive one. We are concerned more with what parents do right than with what they do wrong. What this book does is to help parents better understand what it is they are doing when they are effective, so that they can extend that approach to the situations which are causing them difficulties. Our message to parents is, "You are already very capable—much of the time. You don't have to unlearn everything you believe and feel about your children. You don't even have to learn anything new. Simply understand the technique you use when you are successful and apply that approach to the situations in which you are struggling."

Most other books assume that they know how to raise *your* children; that they know what is best for them. This book will not advise or tell you what kinds of things you should or should not try to get your kids to do. What we do say is, "You have the power as parents to get those behaviors from your children that you desire, but you should choose only those behaviors that are really worth the effort. Do not look upon this technique as a chance to become a dictator in the home. Remember that this approach does not make changing problem behaviors into a fun game. The technique should, therefore, be used with great selectivity."

A most important feature of the book is that Part II describes how parents can put into practice the concepts detailed in the first three chapters. A family intervention work sheet, similar to the one the authors use in family therapy, is presented to enable the reader to clearly see the course of action necessary to correct any difficulty which may be occurring in the parent-child relationship.

It has been very exciting working with families over the last several years applying the principles presented in this book. The reward of helping these families to live together successfully has been extremely fulfilling. We are confident that those who read and apply the concepts in this book will also derive tremendous benefit for their efforts within a short period of time.

Contents

How to Get Your Children to Do What You Want Them to Do

PART ONE

PARENTAL PITFALLS

1 SAYING WHAT YOU MEAN MEANING WHAT YOU SAY

"I cannot get my nine-year-old to go to bed," complained a frustrated parent. "I've tried everything, but no matter what I do, he just won't obey me. Then in school he is always so tired he falls asleep. What am I to do? I've tried spanking him and telling him that he needs to get his rest so he'll do well in school. I even forbid him to watch TV, but nothing works."

The family therapist to which she had come then asked, "Your child must be very tired in the morning. Do you have any trouble getting him up?" "Oh, yes," she replied, "it's nearly impossible to wake him up. Every day it's the same thing. He screams and cries and complains about being too tired, but I finally get him up and off to school." "What do you say to him when he complains about having to get up?" the therapist asked. "I tell him he can't go back to sleep because he has to go to school. Then I usually have to be very firm and tell him to 'get up now and I mean now.'"

This story is a typical example of what this book is all about. Why is it that parents can get their children to do some things which they don't want to do, and yet cannot get them to obey at other times? In the case above, the parent was very effective in getting her child up and out to school, but was unsuccessful at getting him to go to sleep.

Other examples of successful and unsuccessful parenting can be observed quite readily at public places like supermarkets, beaches, sporting events, and so on. In such surroundings you can observe many parents who are extremely effective in controlling and guiding their children's behavior. Other parents, however, may yell at, bribe, or even spank their children and still not get the desired results. Why is the first group so effective in dealing with their children, while the latter group only seems to be successful in getting into one authority battle after another?

The key to getting children to do what you want is revealed by listening carefully to the way in which parents communicate their desires to their children.

The parents who are successful in getting their children to do what they want state their desires in very clear terms, that cannot be misunderstood. Also, they are consistent with these communications. They do not first tell Johnny that he can't have any candy while waiting in line at the supermarket and then give in a minute later to stop his crying. When these parents make up their minds that their child is to do something, they demand that it be done.

On the other hand, parents who are having trouble with their children's behavior communicate quite differently. They do not make demands of their children in the areas which are causing problems. That doesn't mean that they just sit around and let their children misbehave without trying to change their behavior. In fact, these parents often feel as if they have tried everything. But what they have not tried is demanding that their child do what they want. This can be clearly seen in the case of the parent who cannot get her son to bed. She is successful at getting him up in the morning because her communications leave no room for argument. He knows he must get up and that's that. But she doesn't demand that he go to bed at night. She reasons with him and punishes him, but does not insist that he do as she says.

Unfortunately, many parents believe that they are demanding a behavior from their child when in reality they are not. Instead their communications are less directive, and therefore less effective. The use of such communications is Parental Pitfall No. 1.

Consider the following examples of unsuccessful parental communications:

A foster parent reported that her son was frequently truant from school. On other occasions he stayed on the school grounds, but would do things like smoke in the bathroom instead of going to class. "What can I do?" the parent asked. "Nothing I've done has worked at all. I've tried to inspire in him a desire to learn. I've told him how important school is, and that he should get a good education or he'll have a tough time in life. Every day I drive him to school. When I drop him off I tell him to work hard, and to meet me at three o'clock. If when I come back to get him, he has cut school, I either spank him or tell him that he cannot play with his friends for a few days. I have even gone and sat with him in his classroom, but as soon as I'm not there he's up and out again. I can't be with him in school forever. Once when I thought I'd had it with him, I told him that

if he ever cut again I was going to give him back to
the foster agency. Threatening him with that didn't
work either."

The strategies that this woman was employing seemed
to her to be demands that the child not be truant. However, as we shall see in this chapter, none of the methods
she was using conveyed to the child a clear message that
his parent meant for him to go to school, be in his class,
and stay there until after school. Each of her communications illustrates a type of ineffective approach to
behavioral problems.

INSPIRATION, ENCOURAGEMENT, AND MOTIVATION

"I tried to inspire in him a desire to learn"

One thing no one can do, not even parents, is to control
the emotions of another person. You cannot "inspire"
someone to do something. You cannot make someone
"like" something. In fact, parents and others often
waste a tremendous amount of time and energy trying
to "motivate" their children to do what they want them
to do. The assumption behind all these attempts is that
the child will decide to do what the parent wants when
he "feels" like doing them. This "feeling" has been
known to take years to develop.

One example of parents emphasizing emotions as
opposed to behaviors is the case of a father who wanted
his daughter to do her chores, and "to do them cheer-
fully." He wanted her to develop a kind of a "whistle
while you work" attitude. However nice that may be in

terms of creating a pleasant environment around the house, it is patently unrealistic to expect someone to enjoy something she doesn't want to do in the first place.

Another parent wanted not only that her child practice the piano every day, which she hated, but that the child *want* to practice the piano. This issue became a terrible battlefield between them and the result was that the child finally took a hammer to the piano while the mother was out one day. This child, the mother stated, had previously been a perfect child in almost every way. She did well in school, she was wonderful around the house, but when it came to the piano, "I had to sit there in the same room with her and demand that she practice it." The child did what her mother told her, but she never developed a liking for the piano. It is probable that when this girl grows up she, like many others who were forced as children to "like" their instruments, will never touch a piano again.

Likewise, it is difficult to imagine that all the inspiration and motivation in the world would cause the child who is used to cutting classes, failing his school work, and smoking in the bathroom, to well up in the heart with a love for books and academic learning.

It is, therefore, important to keep in mind that whereas parents can demand that their child do something, they cannot demand that their child will want, like, or be inspired to do that behavior.

Interestingly enough, when parents deal directly with the child's problem behavior by demanding that he change, it frequently occurs that the attitude of the child toward that activity also changes in a more positive way.

Such was the case of Arnold, age twelve, who was doing *A* work in mathematics, but was virtually failing every other subject. He had even received special tutoring in these areas to no avail. When his parents came to family therapy, the following dialogue took place:

Therapist: Why is it, do you suppose, that Arnold does so well in one subject, yet seemingly has such difficulty with history, English, and geography?

Father: That's easy. Arnold loves math. He'd rather do his homework in math than watch TV or play outside with the kids. He's a fanatic. Even all of the dice and card games he plays are all math-oriented. He's just a born mathematician, I guess.

Mother: And as much as he adores working with numbers, that's how much he hates all of his other subjects. That's why he never does his homework in those classes. Heaven knows, we've tried to get him interested in history. We've taken him to plays about famous people from the past, we even took a trip to Washington, D.C. But he just doesn't care about that stuff.

Arnold: It's just too hard remembering all those names and dates. All of those people lived so long ago. Who cares about them anyway?

At first it would be easy to conclude that Arnold, no matter what, would never be interested in anything but mathematics. The fact is that Arnold's apparent disdain for history and English was more a reaction to his parents continually trying to "inspire" him in that direction than anything else. Finally his parents realized how fruitless it is to try to manipulate other people's emotions, and instead they decided to just demand that he do his homework in those subjects as well as he did his assignments in math and to just leave Arnold's emotions alone. Several months later, Arnold's parents called to say that Arnold was not only getting *B*'s and *A*'s in *all* of his subjects, but that he was now as enthusiastic about history and English as he had previously been about math.

Of course, not all children would have responded the same way in this situation. Some would have gone right on hating those classes while doing their homework and improving their grades. However, in this case, as in many others we have seen, when the parents focused directly on changing the behavior of the child, his emotions were left free to take care of themselves.

REASONING

"You should get a good education or you'll have a tough time in life"

In addition to trying to inspire her child to want to learn, the foster parent mentioned earlier also tried pointing out some of the important reasons why he should get an education. This had not been successful because if a reason to do something is not backed up with a demand that it be done, then the choice of whether or not to do it is left with the child. Thus, he is allowed to decide from his perspective whether the reason is important enough to him to influence his behavior. The child often develops the viewpoint that he doesn't have to do what his parents want if he can prove that there is a flaw somewhere in their thinking. In the case of telling a child that he will have a tough time in life if he doesn't do well in school, a quick-witted child might respond with examples of various friends or people he has heard about who have been successful even though they dropped, flunked, or were thrown out of school at an early age. The stories of Thomas Edison, Albert Einstein, and Carl Sandburg are frequently employed in this regard.

Reasoning with children often leads to heated discussions or arguments instead of leading to the desired behavior. Through arguing, the child learns that he can at least postpone having to do what his parents want, and on occasion can even get them to back down from or modify their stand. It also tells him that his parents are not really sure about what they believe.

Often, it is appropriate to tell a child what he is to do and then to explain briefly the value or importance of that behavior. However, as the following case illustrates, parents can overdo "explanations," and thereby leave the child totally confused as to what behavior, if any, is expected of him.

> Eight-year-old Jay was brought to the family therapy center by his mother with only one complaint. Every morning Jay tromped through his mother's prize tulip garden on his way to school. Everything else about Jay was perfect. He was an *A* student, president of his class, leader of his scout troop, and loved by everyone. At home he did everything his mother requested with no problems except for the tulips.

Jay's mother was asked, "What do you say to Jay when he leaves for school each morning?" Her reply was, "I say exactly the same thing every morning. Don't walk through the tulips. Those tulips are all imported from Holland and raised in special soil with special feedings each week and I spend at least an hour a day caring for them. Why, you know, there are eighty-four varieties of tulips in that garden, and many of them are thought not even to grow in this part of the country, etc., etc., etc." Jay's mother continued about her prize tulips for five minutes. At the end of her filibuster, Jay was asked what the real point of his mother's talk was, and he said, "There are eighty-four varieties of tulips in the garden which are imported from Holland and they require lots of special care and feeding." Jay's mother then turned to the therapist and said, "People have always said I talk too much. I guess just saying don't walk in my tulips would work better."

It is frequently quite reasonable to explain to a child the why's and how's of doing and not doing certain things. Children who continually hear, "because I said so," in response to every question they ask, not only develop a lot of resentment toward their parents, but also tend to do more poorly in school because they are not used to analyzing or questioning what they read or learn about. They simply accept whatever is presented to them and do not bother to understand the under-lying principles of the material. This limits them to success at tasks which require only such skills as rote memory.

What the authors tell parents about answering their

children's questions is to stop and think whether the child is really asking for information or whether he is stalling for time. It is easy enough to determine this by observing whether the child makes use of the parents' answer or whether he then begins to debate, question, and challenge what he has been told.

There is also a great deal of difference between telling someone what he "should do" and what he "is to do."

> One parent was having a terrible time getting her son to stop hitting his sister. Over and over that child had been told, "You should love your sister. If you loved her you would never hit her." This child had continually been told what he "should do," but he had never been told that he was not to hit his sister again. As was already stated in this chapter, people cannot be made to like or love anything or anyone. In addition, people do all sorts of mean things to those they supposedly love, so expecting love for a baby sister to prevent a child from walloping her once in a while is less than realistic.

A major misconception with "should" statements is that many of us know precisely what we ought to do, but still choose to ignore such ideas and behave in accord with other desires instead. Children are no different in this regard; therefore, when they repeatedly behave inappropriately, parents need to do more than educate them as to what they should do. Furthermore, words such as *love, respect, care,* and *concern* are all very complex and abstract terms. For centuries philosophers, poets, and others have discoursed on and debated about the true meaning of these terms. How, then, can we expect children to understand what man has been unable to define precisely?

WISHES AND DESIRES

"I drive him to school every day"

Driving a child to school is a clear communication that the parent wishes or desires that the child go to school. However, many of our wishes in life just do not come true. Firm steps and concrete action nearly always need to be taken before our desires are made realities. We may get the idea from television game shows, daytime serials, or children's programs, that "wishing on a star" brings immediate and dramatic results from the goodwill of the universe. Certainly dreams and wishes can be an initial step in getting something accomplished. However, if I were sick, I would hope that my doctor would do more than send his best wishes that I get well.

Parents are rarely successful in getting their children to do things when their communications are little more than fond desires. This is particularly true when the child is not concerned about what his parents are desirous of, as might be the case with a foster child who has not been with a family long enough to build up a strong emotional relationship. However, even with children from typical family backgrounds, if the child's desires are as strong as his parents and he is given a choice, his unique sense of justice will favor his own wishes in most cases.

A parent who says, "I want you to do your homework," or, "I want you to be in early tonight," is not telling the child what he is to do. He is simply stating that the parent would like these things to occur. The child may weigh that against what he would like to have occur. There is certainly no sense of urgency or strong commitment in such communications. Therefore, he does not interpret the message as one in which there is but one alternative: that he is to do his homework or to be home at a particular time. He interprets it instead as a flexible statement, and one about which he has the power to make the final decision. Therefore, expressing desires is certainly not the same thing as telling the child what to do and is unlikely to be effective in influencing children's behavior.

VAGUE COMMUNICATIONS

"Work hard and I'll pick you up after school"

After driving the child to school, the foster parent reminded her child to work hard that day and she would pick him up after school. This is a vague communication in that it does not state exactly what the child is to work hard at. To the child "working hard" may mean thinking of a complicated plan for getting out of class or not getting caught in the bathroom. The fact that she has told him that he will be picked up at three o'clock in no way specifies where he is to be until that time. If after being dropped off, this child went to the beach, worked hard at surfing or building a sand castle, and came back to school by three o'clock in time to be picked up, he would in no way have disobeyed his mother's direction. Obviously, telling the child to work hard and to meet her at three o'clock is a vague communication, which demands very little from the child and does not deal at all with his problem behavior. What is interesting is that this parent was always successful in getting her child to be back at school by three o'clock so that he could be picked up. This is because she communicated very clearly that he was to meet her at that time.

Another example of a vague communication is telling a child to "be a good boy." This is a very general and possibly confusing statement, because the meaning of "being good" varies so much from situation to situation that a child would have to be very knowledgeable and experienced with the concept of goodness to clearly understand what his parents mean by the term. Many parents forget that their children's thinking is very immature and that abstract concepts are therefore very difficult, if not impossible, for them to grasp. An example of concrete or literal thinking in children is the story of a mother who, being in a hurry to get her family dressed, told her son, "Take this towel into the bathroom, and you'd better step on it." When she checked up on him a few moments later, she found her child doing *exactly* what she had told him. He was stepping on the towel in the bathroom! Along the same lines, another parent who was having trouble toilet training her six-year-old would tell him to "get in there and sit on that toilet." That is exactly what this child would do. He would sit there every evening until he fell asleep on the toilet.

PUNISHMENTS

"If . . . I find out that he has cut school, I either spank him or tell him that he cannot play with his friends for a few days"

When a child has misbehaved in some way, what is the effect of punishing him? Unless the child is told very clearly that he is not to repeat this behavior, the punishment can be interpreted by the child to mean, "I can do this thing, if I don't mind being punished for it." The child who interprets his punishment in this way would then weigh the advantages of misbehaving versus the disadvantages of the punishment. Often he will decide to gladly pay the price. The crucial point is that the decision is left with the child, not the parent. Parents, in fact, often feel that they have fulfilled their duty by punishing the child, and in this way they have done all they could do to discourage the child from misbehaving. The fact is that they have left the choice and responsibility in the matter with the child.

Frequently, parents ask whether it is helpful to punish the child and at the same time demand that he not repeat a particular behavior. In this case, punishment is really superfluous. It may make the parent feel better to spank or deprive the child of something he enjoys, but it is the parents' demands that alter the child's behavior, not the punishment.

If punishment is ineffective without demands and superfluous with them, it would seem then that punishment may in fact be entirely unnecessary. A television show recently interviewed the author of a book about a newly discovered primitive tribe. When he was questioned as to the tribe's methods of child rearing, he replied that parents never need to employ any punishment whatsoever in dealing with their children. "If a child doesn't do something the first time he is told," the author explained, "his parents will simply repeat more emphatically the original demand. These demands are nearly always all that is required to get children to obey their parents."

When a parent tells a child to go to his room and stay there because he's done something wrong, the punishment may *not* stop the child from doing the misbehavior again, but it does demonstrate that when parents mean what they say, they can get children to do what they want them to do.

One parent was very successful at *punishing* her ten-year-old daughter's bed-wetting. Some days the child had to clean up the bed and launder the sheets. Or she would have to write, one hundred times, "I will try not to wet the bed anymore." Other days she would not be allowed to drink after a certain hour. All of these things the child did, because she was told to do them, but she did not stop wetting the bed because that was one thing she had never been told to do.

THREATS

"Once when I thought I'd had it with him, I told him that if he ever cut again, I was going to give him back to the foster agency, but that didn't work either"

Everyone who has walked a supermarket aisle has heard parents say to their children, "If you touch that again you're going to get it!" Generally, almost before the words are out of the parent's mouth, the child responds by touching the very item he was warned not to handle. Why aren't threats effective in stopping this kind of misbehavior? One major reason is that children learn very early in life that many statements that begin with the word "if" are just meant to scare them, and often never really come true. Phrases such as "if you do that one more time, I'm going to kill you" just are not often followed up, fortunately. Thus, the child learns to play the percentages. Some days his parents will follow through on their threats and some days they won't. It's worth the gamble.

One parent used to say to her child, "If you don't take that trash out, you're going to Juvenile Hall." She had said this to him for months and still he wouldn't take the trash out. When asked if she had ever taken him to Juvenile Hall, this mother replied, "What kind of a parent do you think I am?" She was a lying parent. She didn't say what she meant. Her statement gave the child a choice, it was not a demand. He could either take out the trash or go to Juvenile Hall.

This is the case with all threats. They give the child the power to decide whether he would like to do what his parents want, or to do what he wants and take the the consequences. Like the mother who threatened to take her son to Juvenile Hall, parents often give choices with which they are not really comfortable. If you are going to allow a child to make a decision between two courses of action, then you should first decide that either alternative is acceptable to you. The foster parent mentioned in the beginning of this chapter made the mistake of giving her child the choice between going to school or being sent back to the foster facility. The second choice was clearly not an acceptable alternative. It was to this mother's credit that she would not send her child back because of his cutting school, but her threat only served to show that she was giving a choice to her child which she did not mean to enforce. One parent actually returned her child to a foster agency after a year because the child had lied to her. She had told the child in the beginning that if she ever lied, she would be sent back. This parent had followed through on her threat, but one wonders why the child was given this choice in the first place, and also why the punishment was so severe.

In the following case history the parent made a dramatic mistake in allowing her child a choice she did not really mean to give:

In this instance, 15-year-old Linda had been smoking marijuana, running around with the "wrong bunch of kids," and had been frequently taking off from school after lunch. Things had gotten so bad at home, the parent explained, that Linda had even run away from home the week before, only to be brought home by the police.

As the therapist talked to the parents it became apparent that Linda had very clearly been given the choice to stay at home or run away. This was demonstrated in the kinds of "communications" which her mother and father had repeatedly stated to her. They said such things as, "If you don't like it here, find some place else to live," or, "If we catch you smoking marijuana one more time, we'll send you to boarding school." These parents would never have dreamed that with such statements they were encouraging their daughter to leave. They were making the dual mistake of trying to get her to stop smoking marijuana by threatening to throw her out, instead of demanding that she stop smoking. In addition, they were telling her that if she didn't like the rules around the house, she could leave. When Linda did just that, they were horrified and couldn't understand why their daughter had done such an immature and rash thing.

This is not an unusual occurrence. In a study of over two hundred such runaways, an analysis of the communications parents had made to their children prior to their running away disclosed that *in every case*, there were clear examples of the parents telling the child that it was all right for him to leave. This attitude was communicated by such statements as, "You don't fit in here anymore," "Why don't you go live with your friends if they're so wonderful?" and so on. All of these statements actually encourage and sanction the child's leaving home. Yet the parents are surprised when this occurs because they don't really mean to give the child that choice. However, because they have been ineffective in controlling their child's behavior in other areas, they often unconsciously wish for their child to leave home and thus put an end to the conflict.

Many parents have been applying the principles of several recent books which stress the need for allowing children to experience the "logical consequences" of their actions. As an example of this approach a parent might state, "If you don't wash your dish, then it will be dirty the next time you wish to use it." This can be a satisfactory technique if the parent is happy with either alternative that the child has been presented with; namely, washing the dish or having a dirty one next time. However, most parents would not approve of their child's eating continually off a dirty plate, and they would eventually not tolerate that behavior any longer for fear of the child's physical health.

Even if this approach seems acceptable in the case of a

dirty plate, there are many times when using "logical consequences" seems most illogical. Are parents supposed to sit by and let their children experience the consequences of such actions as running away, drug-taking, stealing, and so forth without first doing everything possible to insure that such behaviors do not occur again?

Certainly, even in homes where parents have been very clear about what they expect, a child may slip up and misbehave. The difference between effective and ineffective parents lies in the way in which they respond to such behaviors. The effective parent will respond in such a way as to emphatically define for the child that he is not to do that behavior again. Letting the child experience the consequences of his actions is simply another way of saying to the child, "You can do this behavior if you are willing to pay the price." It often takes much more than this kind of statement to get a child to change his behavior.

> One child, in the course of serving himself a midday
> snack, dropped a carton of milk on the kitchen
> floor. His mother asked him to clean it up, but he
> said he didn't have time just then and would do it
> later. She said that would be all right, but she would
> not cook dinner until the mess was cleaned up. Hours
> later the job was still not done. Meanwhile, the rest
> of the family had gone out to dinner, but the milk-
> spiller was still in the kitchen putting off cleaning
> up. This parent had given the child a clear choice
> between having dinner by mopping up the mess or
> missing dinner. He was choosing to miss dinner. But
> that choice was not very popular with his mother
> who had to stay with him in the kitchen to see that
> he didn't sneak a piece of food. She obviously was

not happy with the choices she gave him, as few parents would have been. She did not want him to miss dinner. She was simply hoping that the thought of not eating would be a way of manipulating the child into getting him to do what she wanted. Instead of going through this charade, it is more direct and certainly more effective to simply demand that the child do the abhorred behavior and get on with the rest of the day. Parents have better things to do than to invent consequences for behaviors they wish changed. Managing children is already a full time job and there is little justification for complicating the task even more.

Many parents try to encourage their children to do things by offering them rewards. "If you clean your room, you can have the car tonight," or, "if you do your homework, you can watch television." As with all "if" statements, these communications imply that the behavior may not occur; there is only a chance that it will happen and, if it does, then the child gets rewarded for it. A slight modification of the same idea is to change the word "if" to "when." Now the child is told that "when" he is finished with a given task, he will get a particular reward. This implies that there is no choice about doing the task, but that in addition, there is a reward for doing it.

Proponents of behavior modification will also insist that if you give a child a reward for doing something, then the likelihood of his continuing that behavior will be greatly increased. Certainly if the child enjoys the particular reward being doled out by his parents, it is probable that the child will do as his parents wish.

However, this is true only of some children. Other children, no matter how attractive the reward is made, cannot be influenced in this way. The fact is, as we will discuss later in the book, some children are by nature more cooperative than others. In reading of supposed "cures" using behavior-modification techniques, one is struck by the degree of cooperation contributed by the child under treatment. One example cited was the case of a child who was "cured" of sucking her thumb by having to wear a glove every time she did this and getting an ice-cream cone every night after dinner if she hadn't sucked that day. It is obvious that if this child had not cooperated in wearing the glove or wasn't willing to trade her thumb-sucking for ice-cream sucking, she never would have been "cured" using rewards. Time and time again, the authors have seen children whose parents have tried every conceivable bribe and punishment without being able to change their child's behavior one iota. In fact, several children had become very good at "stringing their parents along" by changing with the introduction of a new reward just long enough to reap the benefits of the reward for a little while.

OTHER INEFFECTIVE COMMUNICATIONS

"The Counselor-Parent"

One parent rarely demanded anything from his child; instead this rather intelligent father would attempt to help the child deal with and work through his "feelings." He was being a counselor and therapist to the child, but not a father.

Gene, age ten, was engaging in bizarre and dangerous behaviors. He would often come home from school, run into the house, and start a rampage of destruction. He threw china out the windows, broke furniture, even banged his head against the walls, injuring himself in the process. At school he was not much better. He never played with his classmates; instead he would hover around the teacher, afraid to leave her side.

His father was convinced that all of these problems were related to the fact that "Gene was a very emotional child." Therefore, when his child would go into his daily rage, Gene's father would say things like, "Boy, are you upset today," and "You sure have a lot of anger stored up inside that you need to get out." These communications did little except to reassure Gene that he had good reason to be acting as he was, and that it was both healthy and necessary that he release his pent-up feelings in these ways lest they become bottled up inside.

TRYING TO UNDERSTAND THE CHILD THROUGH QUESTIONING

The father mentioned above who helped his child get out his anger would also ask him all kinds of questions designed to probe the underlying motives behind these behaviors. "Did someone hurt your feelings at school today?" was a typical response to Gene's banging his head against the wall. "Were you mad at mother today?" was the question following Gene's ripping to shreds a dress of his mother's. (The most significant intervention these parents made was that they substituted plastic dishes for the china that Gene had been throwing out the window. They then locked the good dishes in the closet. It would not be surprising if they had even opened the window for him.)

Questions such as these imply to the child that his parents believe he has a good and valid reason for what he is doing. Sure enough, as he recollects his activities, there was an instance or two where in his opinion he had been maltreated. "My parents are right," he says to himself, "I did have a miserable day, and that is why I need to get all of these angry feelings out."

There is no question that children do occasionally feel the need to release or express their negative emotions. However, there is no evidence to suggest that it is particularly helpful to express them through acts of violence or destruction. There are many more constructive outlets for negative emotions. In Gene's case, as with many other children, the problem does not seem to be the child's need to express his feelings, but rather the child is behaving according to the expectations which his parents have made perfectly clear in their communications.

Questioning children as to why they are behaving in a particular way is an especially appealing pastime of parents these days. Its popularity derives, in part, from the notion that if we understand the causes of our behaviors then we will be able to control or change them. Unfortunately, research has not confirmed or verified this idea. The fact is that although insight into the underlying mechanisms behind our behavior may be intellectually stimulating, other factors must also occur before any significant personality change can take place.

Asking a child why he does something not only has very little effect on changing the child's behavior, but often takes the parent on a wild goose chase, because frequently the child hasn't any idea *why* he did what he did, and, in fact, had no good reason at all for his behavior. However, he may feel compelled to invent a plausible explanation because this is what he thinks his parents want.

The following are some of the more common questions parents ask their children followed by typical children's responses:

> *Parent:* "Why don't you sit still?"
> *Child:* "I don't know."
>
> *Parent:* "Why did you hit your little brother?"
> *Child:* "He hit me first."
>
> *Parent:* "What's gotten into you today?"
> *Child:* "There's nothing to do."

All of these questions and answers are really beside the point. Either the parent wants the child to sit still and to stop hitting his brother, or not. If getting the child to stop these behaviors is what the parents really want, then their understanding the reasons behind his doing these things will be of little value to them.

In the case mentioned above where the parents ask the child "What's gotten into you today?" it would be much more effective to state the specific behaviors that the child is engaging in which are bothersome, and then to demand that the child not do those things. When that has been accomplished, the child may wish to offer a reason or excuse for his behavior. He may say, for instance, that he had an argument with his friend at school and that is why he has been picking on his sister. At that time it can be useful to empathize with the child by showing that you understand how he feels. Such statements as, "It's hard when you have a disagreement with a good friend, isn't it?" can be helpful in letting the child know that you understand him. That does not mean that you back down from your demands that the child not misbehave. In fact, it is important to reiterate that even when he feels bad about something he cannot "take it out" on his sister.

REQUESTING THAT THE CHILD CHANGE HIS BEHAVIOR

"Please don't slam the door"

The parent who is always concerned about being a "nice guy," who wants his child to continually like him, is rarely able to demand anything from them and instead resorts to polite requests. The result is that while some children respond to the Mr. Friendly approach, many children interpret it as a sign of weakness and, after due consideration of their parents' appeals, they do just as they wish.

There is certainly nothing imperative in a request. Children are continually asking for things which they do not receive; therefore, it is only reasonable that when parents "ask" them to behave, they in no way feel any obligation to comply with the request.

One parent stated that she always told her child exactly what he was supposed to do, but that he

never listened to her. At that time the child was
playing with some breakable object in the office.
The therapist asked the parent to demonstrate how
she would get her child to stop playing with the
object. She said, "Now dear, wouldn't you like to
play with something else?" The statement was so
potent that the child, who was four, looked at her
for about a second and then continued to play
with his "toy." "There," the parent said, he never
does anything I tell him to do." The therapist then
stated, "I can see how you might think that you
have told your child to do something, but what you
just did was to ask him if he wanted to stop. He
though about it for a minute and then decided
not to."

In another case a recently divorced mother was having a
great deal of difficulty because she presented all of her
communications to her son in the form of requests.

The family therapist visited six-year-old Eric and his
mother at home. When it came time to start the
session, Eric's mother asked him to come and sit on
the couch so that they could begin. He said he didn't
want to. She asked him again and received no
response this time. This went on for quite a while
until the parent made one last attempt at getting
her son to obey. She caught his eye and pleadingly
said, "P-L-E-A-S-E, Eric, come and sit down." Eric,
not wanting to embarrass his mother any further,
finally acquiesced and strolled over to the couch and
sat defiantly with his feet tucked under him, his
shoes pressing hard against the velvet cushion.

It was very clear who was in control in this family, and the communications illustrated this quite convincingly.

If all of the communications discussed thus far are not effective, what is left?

When parents have tried to inspire, reason with, punish, threaten, and plead with their child unsuccessfully, the only alternative remaining for them is to clearly and emphatically *demand* that the child change his behavior. Demands differ from all of the previously discussed communications in that they are emphatic and precise. A case history will illustrate the use of demands:

> Scott, aged twelve, was having great difficulties in a school to which he had recently transferred. Whereas he had been an *A*-minus student at his old school, his grades had fallen to *D*'s and *F*'s, and he was cutting classes as well. Testing showed that he had a rather high IQ. It was therefore felt by the school counselor that Scott had an emotional problem which was causing him to perform badly in school.

> When Scott and his parents came to family therapy, his mother mentioned that she wanted Scott to enjoy school and get along with his teachers and classmates. She thought that he was just like his father in that when he didn't like something, there was "no way on earth" you could get him to do it. Both parents mentioned that they had tried various methods of getting Scott to stay in class and do his homework and not to cut class.

> The therapist then pointed out to Scott's parents: "It seems to you that you have tried everything to

get Scott to stay in school and do his homework. However, the one thing I haven't heard you say is that you have *demanded* that Scott do these things." "But what can we say?" questioned Scott's mother. The therapist then asked her to think of a time when Scott did not want to do something, but she was able to get him to do it anyway. She thought awhile and at first stated that she never could get him to do anything if he really didn't want to. Finally Scott himself interrupted and said, "What about those dumb family picnics you make me go to?" The therapist then asked Scott's mother to remember exactly what she said to her son about his going to the picnics. She stated, "I just tell him, 'You're going.' " The therapist then pointed out that she was very successful in getting Scott to do what she wanted when she made a demand. "However," he added, "no one has demanded, the way you do with family picnics, that Scott go to school and do his homework."

Beginning immediately after this session Scott's parents personally took him to school and insisted that he stay there and do his work. This he did and, within a few weeks, he was enjoying school, doing his homework, and his teacher reported that his grades were excellent.

How do demands differ from all the other things parents say to their children? Essentially, there are only two types of demands. One is that the child stop doing something, and the other is that he begin to do something. In the first category are examples such as:

"Stop hitting your brother."
"Don't play with that in the house."
"Don't pick the cat up like that."
"Stop what you're doing and come to dinner."

Some communications which denote that a child is to begin to do something are:

"Be home at ten o'clock."
"Take out the trash."
"Turn the television off."
"Go to bed now."

There is a most significant difference between these demands and the other types of communications mentioned in this chapter. The difference is that all non-demands leave the choice of whether to do the behavior with the child. When parents ask their child to do something, the child has the choice of whether to comply. When reasoning is the approach, the final decision is left with the child. The same is true of warnings, threats, punishments, and encouragements. Only demands make it clear that there is no choice for the child about the particular behavior.

It may be difficult at first for the reader to accept the idea that children do what is demanded of them by their parents. Every parent, however, can think of particular situations in which their child has been told in no uncertain terms what he is to do or not do. In these cases, the child senses that his parents really mean what they are saying, that there is no choice in the matter, and he does as he has been told. For example, nearly all parents get their children to go to school, to not play in the street, to brush their teeth, to stay off the roof, to take baths, and so on. Many children do not want to do these things and frequently resist and complain about having to do them. But they do these things; the reason being that in these cases parents are quite sure that these things are important and their communications reflect the intensity of their convictions.

Parents may question, "You mean that to demand something of a child, all one needs to do is to use certain words and phrases?"

There *is* something more. However, it is crucial to begin by stating the demand in unambiguous terms. In addition to the words, though, it is also necessary that the child know you really mean what you are saying, and that you are not *asking* him to do something, that you are not *wishing* that he would do it, but rather that you are *telling* him to do it.

Parents differ in the way they speak when they really mean what they are saying. Some parents raise their voices a little, others get a certain look on their faces, still others stand differently or look directly in the child's eye when they speak. Whatever the case, every child learns that there is something his parents do when they mean that he is to do exactly what they say. Think for a moment about the way parents would react to their child stepping out into the street as a car was approaching. They would not ask the child to get back on the curb, they would not tell him that if he doesn't get out of the street he might get hurt. What they would do would be to yell to the child in the clearest and most emphatic terms they know that he is to get back on the sidewalk.

It is often quite natural for parents, in the course of

making demands of their children, to become emotional to some extent. In spite of what some experts say, it is unreasonable to expect that parents not get mad or angry at their children some of the time. Expressing this anger is also an essential part of a meaningful message. The parent who tries to cover up these feelings usually ends up with a powerless communication, because the parental emotions are essential cues which help a child to realize that what has been said has been meant. Without these cues a child may feel that his parents' message is really not that important.

"BUT I DON'T LIKE TO GET MAD AT MY CHILDREN"

Often, however, parents do not want to be the "bad guy," they don't want to scare their child, or hurt his feelings. They may be afraid to express anger lest their temper get out of control. There is something about anger which frightens many parents. It is an emotion about which they are particularly uncomfortable. They will go to any lengths to avoid it. For them an angry confrontation is about the worst experience imaginable. In dealing with their children, they will try to quietly talk over everything as if engaged in a summit talk with the great heads of state. This approach, unfortunately, just does not work with many children. They nod their heads in agreement and seem to understand and appreciate every word, yet five minutes later are engaged in the same unacceptable behaviors.

The reason for this is that in trying to remain calm, the parent sends a message which seems less than imperative. It becomes just another statement without any real potency. Therefore, the child tends to think that he can probably get away with not doing what he has been told. In the end, the parent who wanted to control his temper usually ends up losing it anyway because the child has not done what was wanted. Only at this point the parent explodes and does something ineffective (but tension-releasing), such as telling the child off or spanking him.

On occasion, a completely frustrated parent may even abuse a child physically. Most of these parents simply do not know any other way to deal with their children's problem behaviors. Their anxiety about not being able to control their children grows and grows until the anger and frustration which they have been trying to control comes out in a dangerous and tragic manner. What these parents and all parents need to understand is that one does not have to resort to such drastic steps in order to control a child's behavior. Instead, if parents would realize that they can be effective with their children by virtue of their own parental power, they would not be so intimidated by challenges to that authority. When parents are confident in their ability to head a family, the child senses this and does not enter into authority battles nearly as often as in families where the parents are not sure of, or comfortable with, the parental role.

Oftentimes parents are made to feel that it is not good parenting to demand things of children in an angry tone. An example of "trying to be nice" by controlling anger occurred at the beach:

Four children between the ages of eight and twelve were playing ball against a retaining wall. The ball continually went out of control causing the children to chase it, with the result that many people had sand kicked onto their blankets or bodies. Some people just missed being hit by the fast-moving tennis ball. One person attempted to influence the children's behavior. At first, she tried to reason with them by saying that this was a public beach and "you have to respect other people's rights." Predictably, this was met with four heads nodding in agreement then immediately returning to play ball.

In a short time, this same person awoke to find the ball at her head, and three children diving all around her trying to retrieve it. She then threatened to tell the lifeguard if they bothered her again. This statement had more effect than the first, but several minutes later they were back. She finally stood up and told them to get away from her. This time she did not try to reason with the children or threaten them. She did not try to remain calm and control herself or ignore the behavior as everyone else was doing. She allowed herself to express her angry feelings which she justifiably felt after a succession of interruptions and disturbances, preventing her from enjoying the beach.

As was stated, none of the other adults on the beach reacted at all to this invasion of their rights. In fact, when the girl raised her voice, some thought she was acting intolerantly and being unfair. "Children can't understand the idea of public rights, they don't know any better, they are only playing," were some of their comments. It was obvious that the girl had restrained herself from losing her temper for so long because she had absolutely no support from the other people present.

In addition to avoiding anger, there are other reasons why parents do not want to express negative emotions to their children. The term "negative" is in itself an indication that anger, sadness, and jealousy are "bad" emotions and should be kept in the closet if possible. Parents, in particular, have been led to believe that expressing their emotions can be damaging to children. It is often implied that the ideal parent is one who is almost always easygoing, who handles children with unending kindness and patience, and who manages to stop inappropriate behaviors while at the same time showing the child that he is still a fine person. It is not unusual to encounter parents who proudly state that they have never had to "raise their voice to their children." This would be great were it not for the fact that these same parents frequently experience significant behavioral problems with their children.

As the following case history demonstrates, it is sometimes necessary for parents to express anger to their children in order to more fully communicate that they mean what they are saying:

Jacqueline Peters, aged seventeen, was at the time of her referral confined to the hospital. She had been diagnosed as having *anorexia nervosa.* This is a medical term for a condition wherein the person is unable to eat due to nausea and vomiting at the ingestion of food and therefore gradually loses weight, becoming weak and dangerously ill. In Jacqueline's case, she had been experiencing these difficulties for three months and had finally lost so much weight that it was necessary for her to be tube-fed and so she was ordered by her family physician into the hospital.

The doctors there told her parents that they should be very loving and kind to their daughter, and that the staff would be the "bad guys" and try to force her to eat. However, this procedure did not work at all, and as a last resort the family was referred for psychological help. The therapist refused to see Jacqueline or her family in the hospital. It was felt that since there was no medical basis for her difficulty, treating her as a sick patient would merely play into the idea that the problem was something outside the child's and parents' ability to control. The family arrived at the office with Jacqueline so weak that she was brought in in a wheel chair. "She says that she wants to eat," her father stated, "but that she just can't keep any food down." After much discussion the therapist pointed out that no one had demanded that Jacqueline eat her food. "Demanded it?" her mother asked. "Of course we've told her to eat." The therapist then pointed out that the parents had begged, punished, and threatened Jacqueline but that they had, in fact, never demanded that she eat. The parents by this time were so desperate that they were willing to try anything. That night Jacqueline's father told his daughter that since she had no physical problems which could prevent her from eating, she was to join them for breakfast the next day and eat what was put on her plate. The morning came and Jacqueline promptly locked herself in the bathroom. Her father then stated that if she did not open the door he would break it down and physically take her downstairs to the table. She would not open the door, so her father demonstrated that he meant what he said by breaking down the door. He then marched his daughter downstairs where she ate the food on her plate and kept it down as well.

During the following week, Jacqueline's parents made it very clear at each meal that she was to eat everything on her plate, and this she did. The next time the family saw the therapist, the only complaint they had was that Jacqueline had not gained much weight back. The reason for this, it turned out, was that since their daughter had not eaten for such a long time, Mr. and Mrs. Peters thought they should go easy with the portions they gave her. After realizing that they could just as well demand she eat more, they increased the portions and Jacqueline rapidly began to regain her weight and strength.

This case conveys the idea that in order for children to respond to their parents' demands, it is often necessary that the communications be forceful and that they reflect the parents' genuine emotions. In rare cases, this may involve being angry enough to break a door down. More frequently, a firm tone and serious look will effectively indicate to the child that the parents' message is one that is deeply felt and meant.

Of course there may be occasions when children do not respond to their parents' clear and emphatic demands. This may occur especially when a child has been into a particular behavioral pattern for a long time and suddenly his parents demand that he change. Initially, the child may figure that his parents have read another book on raising children and hope that they'll forget about it in a few days. The test as to whether his parents really mean what they are saying comes when he does not do as he is told. What do his parents do then? Do they return to their old, ineffective communications—those that offer the child alternatives, that punish but do not demand, that question the child's reasons for misbehaving, that label the child's behavior, and so on? Or do they stick with demanding the behavior again and again until the child realizes that he has no alternative in this matter; that his parents really mean that he is to change and that he can change?

The latter course of action, namely repeating the demand to the child, is the only choice for the parent who has decided what his child can and will do. The parent who repeats his demands gets results. Some children change overnight, some within two or three days, others with long-term behavioral problems may take between one or two weeks.

One child, twelve-and-a-half, had soiled himself virtually every night of his life. His parents had done all the usual things to try to correct this problem. They had even had a doctor check to see if there were any physiological problems. There were none. When it was pointed out by the therapist that they had done everything but demand that the child stop soiling, they decided right then and there that there was no reason why they shouldn't do this.

They went home and demanded that their child was never to soil himself again.

When he awoke the next morning, he was soiled as usual. They immediately called the therapist and questioned him as to what they should do next. The therapist asked them what choices they had. They replied that there was really no other alternative but to repeat their demand. That day and for the next three days, both in the morning and at bedtime, their communication was the same. They firmly restated their belief that he was capable of controlling himself and since there was no reason for him to soil he was not to do it anymore. It took them five days of doing that to get their child to stop soiling the bed after twelve-and-a-half years of his doing so.

PHYSICAL REINFORCEMENT

With some behaviors it is possible for parents to reaffirm the fact that they mean what they are saying through physical as well as verbal means. Physical reinforcement is not to be confused with physical punishment or hurting the child in any way. An example of physical punishment would be: a parent tells his child to go to bed and then spanks the child when he does not do as he is told. The parent in this case has sent a clear message: "I did not mean that you had to go to bed. What I meant was that if you don't go to bed you get a spanking." A parent who uses physical reinforcement instead of punishment would take the child to his bedroom and even place the child in bed, if necessary. By doing this a parent is saying, "I really meant it when I said that you have to go to bed." The child in this case learns that when his parents say something, they back it up.

There are many examples of behaviors which can be affected through the use of physical reinforcement. Everyday examples of such parenting include: picking a child up and bringing him back within the limits of the yard in which he is playing; personally taking a child who often has been truant to school; turning the TV off when the child refuses to do so. All of these acts signify to the child that his parents mean what they say. They are not enacted in such a way as to connote to the child, "See, I'm bigger and stronger than you." Rather, the parent simply uses the minimum amount of force necessary to communicate that this is something the child has to do.

CHILDREN'S MANIPULATIONS

In parent-child relationships where parental communications are meant, the child soon learns that it is a waste of time to try to con his parents into letting him have his way. His parents may be flexible to the extent that they can be reasoned with, but he knows that they will not respond to manipulative behaviors such as pouting, procrastination through arguing, complaining about lack of parental love, or comparisons with what other children are allowed to do.

Marshall, a seriously overweight ten-year-old boy, was an effective manipulator. His father stated that several times he had put the child on a diet, but that none of them had worked because his son would always "scream to high heaven about how he was being starved to death, and that if we loved him we would not be doing this to him." The father further stated that it was so hard to "look into his eyes and see those tears." (One would have thought that it would also be difficult to look at the dangerously obese body of his child as well.)

In this example, the parent was not willing to tolerate his child's apparent sadness at being deprived of food. Other parents may not be able to tolerate their child's anger. When a child becomes aware of this, he learns that he can get his way by withholding his affection or by stating that he no longer loves his parents. Instead of interpreting such proclamations as a child's natural reaction to frustration or as manufactured feelings, parents often take the child's words personally. Thus, they seriously worry about whether their child will reject them (as if a child could deliberately cease to love his parents for very long). The child, in these cases, has the power in the family. He controls his parents and can avoid their demands by forcing them to back down through the use of his emotions.

Children who are successful at manipulating their parents in these ways grow up to think the rest of the world will probably respond just as easily to their complaints. Often, they are quite disappointed and surprised that the world will not so easily adjust its standards to accommodate them.

Should parents ignore their child's crying and complaining? In some cases, ignoring the child's response is the most suitable and effective thing to do. Other times, a parent may want to show that he is aware of how the child is feeling, but that in spite of those feelings, the child still has to do what he has been told.

For example, a child who is told to clean up his room may complain that all of his friends have messier rooms than he, that he never gets to play because he has to clean up all the time, that it is too big a chore, and so on. The parent can empathize with the child by saying, "I know this is something you dislike doing, that you feel it is unfair that you have to do it, and that you are angry at me for making you clean it up. I can understand all this, but this is still your job and you are to do it." Any more discussion than this would be futile and would serve only to delay the child from his getting started on the project. When parents reflect the feelings of their children in this way, they are, in fact, saying, "It's okay to not like doing what you have to do. It's even all right that you don't like me at the moment. I can accept those things." In this way, the child learns that his parents are at least interested in his feelings even though they will not back down from their expectations for him.

In this chapter we saw that parents can be very effective in getting their children to do what they want when their communications make it clear that the child has no choice in the matter and that his parents really mean what they say; that they will follow through on their demands.

Parental Pitfall No. 1 occurs when parents use communications which are not demands, such as the following: Trying to inspire or encourage the child to do something; trying to reason with the child; using vague words and phrases; punishing the child; using threats and warnings; interrogating the child; pleading that the child do·what he is asked. These communications are rarely effective in changing problem behaviors.

The "magic" of demands lies both in the preciseness of the words used so that there is no room for misunderstanding, and in the way these words are communicated. When demands are stated clearly and meaningfully, the result almost always is that the child does exactly as he has been told.

It was pointed out that sometimes making demands involves getting angry. Other times physical reinforcement is required. In addition, parents must learn to deal with and avoid being entangled by their children's manipulations to get out of doing what has been demanded of them.

2

ESTABLISHING CLEAR GOALS FOR YOUR CHILD

The second pitfall, as the chapter title implies, is that parents very often have not clearly established, have lost sight of, or are in conflict over their own parental values.

When parents are not sure of or are vague about what they want their children to do, their communications are necessarily vague also. The following case demonstrates the relationship between clear parental values and clear communication:

Todd, aged ten, was having serious problems in school and with the law. For these reasons his parents brought him to family therapy. When Todd's mother was asked to describe the kinds of things she said to her child each day before he went to school, she stated, "I always tell him to have a nice day." On the surface, of course, this seems like a friendly enough and appropriate message. But for a child like Todd, whose daily pastimes included stealing and other objectionable activities, this was not the kind of communication he required. For him, "having a nice day" included being successful at pilfering great amounts of candy and other children's lunch money. When he did this, he probably felt that we was in no way disobeying his mother's morning send-off.

It is clear from this example that Todd's mother needed to communicate to her child in more specific terms. For her to do this, she would first have to clarify her goals for her child. She needed to ask herself what she wanted Todd to do during the day besides enjoy himself. After realizing that her goals had been vague in her own mind, and that therefore her communications to her son had been equally vague, she began to specify her expectations. She reflected and decided that she wanted Todd to "sit in his classroom and do his work and not take anything from others." This proclamation is a long way from the well-meaning, but meaningless statement, "Have a nice day."

A METHOD FOR HELPING PARENTS ESTABLISH OR CLARIFY THEIR GOALS FOR THEIR CHILDREN

Step 1 / *Specifying Problem Behaviors*

In helping parents to establish goals for their children, we have found that a good place to begin is by asking them to describe the kinds of things their children are doing that trouble them. In the course of doing this, parents will frequently label their child's behavior in vague and general terms, such as emotionally disturbed, hostile, sad, moody, or stubborn. Because these terms mean different things to different people, and therefore communicate very little about what the child is actually doing, the parent is questioned further until he focuses on the specific problem behaviors.

The following case history demonstrates how, through this process, parents can develop clear goals for their children.

Jeffrey, aged eight, was brought in by his mother who described him as a "depressed child." "What is it that he does that makes you believe that he's depressed?" the therapist asked. Her response, as it is with many parents who described their children's behaviors in generalities, was to avoid the idea that her child did anything specific to indicate that he was depressed. "He just doesn't enjoy life," was her comment. However, further questioning revealed that what Jeffrey did was to "come home from school, sit in the corner, and essentially do nothing." "He doesn't go outside and play with the other children on the block," his mother stated. "He's isolated himself, and I'm afraid he's going to end up in a mental institution."

Thus, this mother began to see that the reason she viewed her son as a depressed child was because he engaged in specific behaviors that seemed inappropriate to her. By clarifying the behaviors which were of concern to her, Jeffrey's mother had established clear goals for her child. She was then in a position to face, head-on, the issue of communicating to her son that he change these behaviors. This she did by demanding in clear and meaningful terms that he go outside and play and stop sitting in the corner. Two weeks later his mother stated that Jeffrey no longer appeared to be depressed. "In fact," she jokingly complained, "I'm now having trouble getting him to come inside."

The reason Jeffrey's mother was so successful was that she stopped seeing her child's behavior in vague terms, and instead focused on the specific things that he was doing which bothered her. Knowing exactly what behavior she wanted changed, enabled her to clearly communicate her expectations to her son.

It is important to remember that parents will differ regarding the goals or values they have for their children. No experts can or should tell you what is best for your child. You have every right to decide what the rules of living should be in your family as long as you are willing to pay the price to see that they are carried out. One set of parents may wish their child home at a certain hour, while other parents of a child of the same age may choose a different time. Does this mean that one parent is right and the other wrong? Of course not. It simply means that each family has its own schedule by which it functions. There cannot be one absolute rule to cover all families. And so it goes with other behaviors. Some parents may decide that their child should be able to smoke at home by a certain age; another family may find the idea totally unacceptable. Some parents may allow their child to wear good clothes to school. Other parents may insist that the child save those clothes for special occasions. These decisions must be made by individual parents. There is no one "right" way. No one has the opportunity to know your family's needs or your children better than you. You are the expert in your house.

Step 2 / *Ranking Parental Goals*
What can parents do if there are ten or twenty things that their child is doing that trouble them? Since it would be impossible to change all of these behaviors at once, parents must decide which behaviors they consider to be of the utmost importance. Having made the decision about which behaviors are *really* important and

must be changed, the next step is for parents to arrange these goals in their order of significance. What typically occurs is that once parents successfully alter their child's behavior in one or two areas that are most crucial, the child experiences his parents as meaning what they say. He then changes, on his own, many of his other misbehaviors, as well as his attitude toward his parents.

This phenomenon is illustrated in the case of Gene, aged ten, mentioned previously. His father was empathizing with rather than demanding anything of his child who was engaging in many unacceptable behaviors, such as refusing to go to school, not playing with his peers, and throwing tantrums at bedtime. His parents set as their first goal getting him to go to school and stay there. The first step was for his mother to take him into the classroom and demand that he stay there until he was picked up. He did this. The next day he was told to take the bus by himself to school. This he also did. Gene's parents then started working on getting him to play with friends. Within a short period of time this was accomplished also. A month later they stated that Gene had stopped doing all of the other unacceptable behaviors they had complained about totally on his own—without any pressure from them.

THE PRICE PARENTS PAY

Sticking with a demand in the face of a child's mumbling and grumbling is no fun. As one parent put it when she began to follow through on her demands, "I'm not very popular with my kids this week." What this parent had learned was that demands are successful, but there is a price that one pays for using them. That price may include your having to get angry or having the child be angry; having to follow through in making sure that the child is doing as told; having to stand one's ground when grandparents, neighbors, and others disagree with your position.

All of this is real work. It is therefore essential that parents only use demands with great selectivity. In order to do this, parents must differentiate between the behaviors that they feel are essential for the child to do, and those behaviors about which the child has some degree of choice. It may be helpful to draw up a list of the crucial behaviors. These can be presented and explained to the child. What is *not* on the list should be considered the prerogative of the child. Thus the child is told what is off limits and what is not. He knows exactly what his parents' values are. In this way he is given the message that there are some things which his parents feel they need to decide for him, and there are also some things about which they feel he has the ability and maturity to make the final decision.

Every child needs and wants to exercise his own autonomy and individuality. To do this he must have the freedom to make choices in some areas of his life. Each parent has to decide for himself in what areas he feels comfortable allowing the child free choice. Too many parents needlessly try to control every aspect of their children's lives. The child is watched over and corrected every step of the way. This smothers the child's sense of worth and causes parents to spend all their time and energy on behaviors that are not really that essential. If you find yourself continually hassling with or nagging your children, then you probably need to distinguish between those behaviors that are important and those that are not of any real consequence. This doesn't mean that if, for instance, you allow your daughter to choose her own color combinations in dressing, you cannot question whether a particular combination might be offensive to some people. The point is that once you give your opinion, the decision is left with the child if that is an area you have allowed for independent decision-making.

Parents often hassle quite needlessly over getting their children to eat their food. If you find yourself becoming enraged every night at the dinner table, ask yourself: Is my child starving to death? Is he malnourished and developing some disease because of his eating habits? Is it really necessary that I get on his back about this? It may well be that the child is not eating up to your highest expectations; but is a perfect diet worth the price of continually checking upon on the child? Some parents may be willing to pay the price. Others may decide that enough is being required of their child already. We are not advising that you back down on those behaviors which you have thought about and feel are of prime importance. However, it is important to keep in mind the difference between those behaviors which you might *prefer* your child to do, and those that you feel are *imperative*. A parent may prefer that his child take up basketball rather than some other sport. However, if the child chose to be on the track team, that parent would probably not order that he quit and play basketball instead. Some behaviors may not be negotiable. These are the parents absolute values. These, of course, will vary from parent to parent, but may include such things as not stealing, doing required chores, coming in at specified times, and so on. A successful parent-child relationship seeks a balance of parent-decided behaviors and child-decided behaviors. If this balance could remain the same throughout childhood, the job of parenting would be a much easier one. But children are continually developing both mentally and physically. This makes it necessary for parents to constantly readjust the authority-autonomy balance in their relationship. This can only be accomplished by reevaluating and redefining the areas in which the ever-maturing child is capable of making his own decisions.

The process of continual reevaluation of a child's capabilities requires parents to observe their child's demonstrated levels of responsibility in various areas of functioning, and then to apply this knowledge as situations arise which require parental decisions. If, for instance, a child is asking to stay out until midnight after a school dance, the parents would need to consider how their child has behaved with previous responsibilities of a similar nature. Did the child come home at the expected time the last time he or she was out late? If this is the first late "date," how has the child handled the responsibility of time in coming home from school or other engagements? This is simply to say parents must look at their child's track record in the area being considered and make the most reasonable decision possible. When a child asks to go down the street to play at a friend's house, a parent's decision must be based on that child's previous street behavior. Does he trample on the neighbor's flowers? Does he stay out of the street? Is he reliable about doing what he says he is going to do? If you ask these kinds of questions when faced with decisions, your understanding of your child's actual capabilities will become clear and subsequent decision-making will be much easier.

FOCUSING ON THE REAL PROBLEM

Sometimes parents may be concerned about a particular behavior, but choose a goal which does not address itself directly to the problem. A common example of this is when parents focus more on "why" the child is doing something than on getting him to change his behavior. It would seem quite appropriate in this day and age where we analyze everything people say and do to determine the motivation and reasons behind a child's misbehavior. Indeed many schools of psychology have taught that only by understanding the deep-seated reasons for one's behavior can we then change. Our approach is quite the contrary to this. We have found that dwelling on the causes of a child's misbehavior results in a lot of guess-work and speculating, and mainly serves the purpose of giving everyone involved, including the child, a good reason for expecting the behavior to continue. This is so because as long as you are discussing "why" the behavior exists, the behavior naturally has to continue to exist or you would have nothing to talk about. That may sound a bit like double-talk, but the fact is that a large percentage of parents come to family therapy seeking not to change a problem behavior, but rather to understand how and why it developed. To these parents we always respond, "In addition to understanding why your child does what he does, do you also wish to change his behavior?" They are not at all the same goals. At this point, the parent will usually respond that they do want to change the behavior, of course. But, as you know by now, the original communications of the parent indicate that they have not been ready to deal directly with this child's misbehavior because they have been occupied with its cause.

The following case history demonstrates these points:

> Bryan, aged six, would not learn to swim even though he had a pool at home. His parents thought it was very important that he do so, in order to prevent an accidental drowning in case he ever fell into the pool. They also wanted him to be able to share in the family fun, much of which centered around frolicking in the pool with brothers, sisters, and neighbors. Bryan, however, persistently avoided the pool and threw tantrums any time someone would mention the idea of learning to swim.

> For some time, his parents had been dealing with this situation by focusing on the "whys" of Bryan's avoidance of the pool. They explored such possibilities as, "Possibly Bryan is afraid that if he goes in the pool his older brothers and sisters may gang up on him and hurt him"; "Maybe he has a fear of water"; "Maybe he's jealous of his brothers and sisters who are already better swimmers than he." To all of these great insights on the part of his parents, Bryan would respond that those were not the reasons. He would only reiterate that he did not like the pool particularly. It seemed that Bryan's parents were convinced there was some deep-seated psychological reason for his not liking the pool, and they were going to discover that reason if it took lengthy

and intensive psychotherapy to do it. Luckily for Bryan and his parents' pocketbook, the therapist helped them to see that Bryan just did not care a great deal for the pool, and that if it was important to them that he learn to swim, they could handle that behavior in the same way they had dealt successfully with any problem behaviors they had experienced with their children.

One day shortly thereafter, Bryan's parents decided that he must learn to swim. So with the money they had saved on psychotherapy, they hired a patient and kind swimming instructor who held fast against Bryan's disdain for the water and finally succeeded in teaching Bryan how to swim. Bryan never did come to enjoy the pool, but at least his parents and he could relax from the daily assault on the inner workings of his nonaquatic-oriented mind.

Another indirect goal centers on getting children to "*learn* to do things." For example, Ruth Ann, aged seven, would not stay in her seat at school. Instead she would try to sharpen her pencil, go to the bathroom, or visit with her classmates. The logical goal would seem to be to get Ruth Ann to sit still in her class. However, her father stated that his goal was that she "learn" to sit still in class.

Is there any difference, you might ask, between the two statements? Yes, for several reasons. First of all, the fact that a person has learned to do something does not in any way guarantee that he will continue to do that thing. Many a piano sits untouched for years by people who have "learned" to play it. Secondly, even if Ruth

Ann's difficulty was that she hadn't learned how to sit still, how would one approach teaching her this skill? By showing her movies of people demonstrating the art of chair sitting? Obviously, the direct and clear goal in this case would be that Ruth Ann sit in her chair at school.

The parental desire that a child "try" to do something is another indirect goal which does not focus on the real problem.

To object to this goal would almost seem "un-American." Is not one of our fondest sayings, "If you don't succeed, try, try again?" What about *E* for effort? Sentimentality aside, the fact is that *trying* to do something is not the same thing as doing it. If in the morning we all just "tried hard" to get out of bed and go to work, chances are, for all our trying, we might not be able to make it a large percentage of the time. In fact, if you observe the use of the phrase, "I'll try," you will find that it is one of the greatest predictors that a person means he will probably not be able to do that thing. Moreover, telling a child that *trying* is all that is expected of him conveys the attitude that the parent does not really believe that the child can actually accomplish the behavior or task.

The final indirect goal which we will deal with has to do with "lying." No, we are not going to advise you that children should be allowed or encouraged to lie. The reason that lying is an indirect goal and does not focus on the real problem is demonstrated in the next case history:

> Twelve-year-old Robert's parents were very concerned about many of the things he was doing. His father stated that he was particularly concerned

about his child's lying. "What kinds of things does he lie about?" the therapist asked. "Well, he's always cutting classes, and one time we knew that he had done it because his teacher had called us, but he still denied it and said the teacher must have made a mistake." The therapist then asked, "If you were successful at getting Robert to stop cutting class once and for all, do you think he would continue to lie about it?" "Why no," his father replied. "He wouldn't have anything to lie about." The therapist continued by saying, "Then it seems very important that you clarify which goal is the most important to you; getting Robert to stay in class or getting him to tell the truth about cutting class. His parents thought for a moment and realized that the real issue at stake was Robert's staying in class, and they proceeded to implement that decision.

Thus Robert's parents learned that a child only lies when he has something to lie about. The issue of lying is one of the most common and upsetting of children's misbehaviors that parents complain about. Parents often get so distraught over their child's lying that they lose sight of the behavior about which he is lying. A tremendous amount of energy and emotion gets poured into telling the child what an awful and deceitful person he is because he has not told the truth. Often parents will tell the child that if he admits his crime (something they usually already know he has done), they will reduce the punishment they have in store for him. They do not recognize that in doing this they are really telling their child to keep on doing the problem behavior but to tell the truth about it.

PARENTS WITH CONFLICTING GOALS

Sometimes parents have difficulty in establishing clear values for their children because they are torn between two goals which are in conflict with one another.

Such was the case with Calvin who was continually getting into fights at school. His parents did not know at first what to do about this situation because they wanted him to stand up for himself, but were also concerned that if he continued his fighting he would be thrown out of school. They were able to resolve this conflict by deciding that he should not fight at school any longer, but that if he was provoked he could beat up the child that had picked on him by arranging to meet him away from school on the way home.

Another family was also having a conflict over two values. It was their chore to decide which one was more important in certain situations.

Carla's parents felt that she was a very curious child of five, and they wanted to encourage her interest in exploring things. However, Carla, in the course of her exploration, had broken much of her parents' furniture and other personal property and this her parents did not like. In resolving this conflict, they had to decide to limit the extent to which "curiosity" would be considered the highest value for their family life. They decided that from that time on only certain areas of the house were acceptable for exploration, and that the rest of the house was off limits. In this way, both values were reconciled.

What about when parents disagree concerning what a child should do? The important thing here is for both parents to sit down and look at what they are saying to their child. It frequently occurs that one parent is saying something like, "clean up your room, it's a mess," and then the other parent says, "oh, leave him alone, he's only a kid." Of course, the child examines the sum total of the parents' communication and decides that he certainly doesn't have to clean up his room.

It is apparent that what is going on in this situation is that one parent is negating the direction of the other. Frequently, the "sabotaged parent" strikes back by undercutting something that is of importance to the other parent. Obviously, the child in such cases is continually exposed to conflicting messages and therefore his behavior cannot please both parents. So he is placed in the position of deciding which parent's message he will obey. This is quite threatening to the child in that he needs and desires both of his parents' approval. The only recourse in such situations is for the parents to allow each other to demand those behaviors which are of vital concern to them. This means that they must sort out those behaviors which are trivial and inconsequential from those that hold special significance for them. It means that parents must respect each other's desires to the extent that they do not interfere with or negate one another's demands.

It is natural that two people living together will inevitably have varying ideas as to what their child should or should not do. However these differences, rather than being sources of conflict, can broaden the goals that they have for their child. For example, a mother may stress school performance; a father may emphasize that the child have responsibilities at home. A child living in such an environment may have many expectations placed upon him. However, if they are realistic, he is in a much better position than a child who is in a situation where he is confused about what he is to do, because pleasing one parent means displeasing the other.

Conflicts also occur when single mothers move in with their parents. Often the grandmother becomes the "nice old lady" whom the child runs to with passionate evidence of unfair treatment at the hands of his mother. If the grandmother sides often enough with the child, this can usurp the mother's authority. One parent found living with grandparents particularly difficult due to the fact that they could not tolerate any crying from her infant child. As a result, the mother stopped making demands of the child so that he would not get upset and cry. Because of this the child became increasingly difficult to handle. One night he became so enraged when he was not allowed to play with a knife that he stabbed his mother with it. Fortunately the wound was not severe, and his parent realized that she could not raise her child in that environment any longer.

WHEN PROFESSIONALS LABEL YOUR CHILD

Another problem in determining goals occurs when parents are told by teachers, counselors or other professionals that there is something wrong with their children.

One parent who had come to discuss her child said that
the principal at her son's school had told her that her
son was "*un*corrigible." The therapist wondered if the
mother understood what that term meant. Upon questioning her, he realized that she had no idea what the
principal had meant, except that it was bad. She could
not communicate clear messages to the child about
his behavior until she had determined exactly what it
was that he was doing that made him "incorrigible."

In another case, the parents of an eight-year-old boy,
Roger, stated that their child's teacher had told them
that their son was "hyperactive." The therapist questioned the ability of a teacher to determine that a child
is hyperactive since it is a medical term, which requires
various tests of a technical nature. The parents were
then encouraged to ask the teacher to describe the
specific things the child was doing that led to his being
viewed as hyperactive. The teacher then explained that
although Roger was doing well in his academic work,
he was a behavior problem in the classroom. "His attention span is extremely short, and he wanders aimlessly
around the classroom and gets himself into trouble."

The therapist then questioned Roger's parents to see
if his attention span and wandering were also a problem at home. "Oh no," exclaimed his mother, "he's
always engrossed in something. He likes reading
books and Saturday mornings he watches TV for
hours." "This certainly is not the behavior of a
hyperactive child," the therapist explained. Roger's
parents agreed with this and, instead of seeing their
child as hyperactive, they began to focus on his

particular problem behaviors and demanded that he do his work at school and stop wandering around the class. "But I finish my work so quickly and then there's nothing to do," replied Roger to his parents' demands. Roger's parents then worked with his teacher to ensure that when he finished his assigned work, he would be directed to other constructive activities and projects in the classroom. Within a short period of time, Roger's apparent "hyperactivity" was a thing of the past.

Whenever children are labeled in various ways by "professionals," it is extremely important that parents find out exactly what the child is doing that has led to his being labeled in this way. Only then can parents formulate goals which are necessary to changing the child's behavior.

Parental Pitfall No. 2 occurs when parents have not carefully analyzed what, specifically, their child is doing that is of concern. To avoid this parents must define the precise behaviors they want changed and not use broad labels such a depressed, moody, hostile, and other such terms which mean different things to different people and cannot be accurately observed.

It is also important that parents rank the goals they have for their child. To change behaviors requires a great deal of effort; therefore only those behaviors worth the effort should be listed. In addition, both parents must agree to support each other in changing the problem behavior.

Parents must focus on the behavior itself and not on

indirect goals such as understanding the source of the problem or getting the child to "*try* and change his behavior."

3 VIEWING YOUR CHILD AS CAPABLE OF CHANGING HIS BEHAVIOR

In the last chapter we saw that parents can avoid Parental Pitfall No. 2 and successfully deal with their children's behavioral or emotional problems by first focusing on the specific objectionable actions of their children, and then demanding that these behaviors be changed.

Parental Pitfall No. 3, which is the subject of this chapter, occurs when parents have come to see their child's misbehaviors or emotional problems as something over which he has no control. In these cases the child is viewed as incapable of changing his behavior. Therefore, parents do not demand that the child do as they wish, since it would be absurd to tell a person to do something that he is felt to be incapable of doing.

This chapter shows that parents are often mistaken in viewing their children as unable to control themselves or act differently. These invalid assumptions must be challenged if the parent is to demand that the child change his behavior.

In the following case history a parent questioned the beliefs which she had about what her child was capable of doing. As a result, her daughter's behavior was affected in a most dramatic way.

Ginger was twelve years old. At the age of six she had been tested and placed in a class for children with low IQ's. During the following years she had performed in school at a level one would expect of a child with far less than average intelligence. However, Ginger's mother began to question the limits of her daughter's capabilities, because at home her child seemed to function quite well.

Ginger often took care of her younger brother and sister, she was able to follow recipes, she ran errands for her mother, and did many things which did not seem to fit with her testing and school performance. At this same time Ginger's mother learned from a friend about some of the ideas we have talked about in this book. She then decided to demand more from her daughter in regard to her work at school. She also went to school and requested that Ginger be assigned homework. The teacher stated that it was not the school's policy to assign extra work to children from "special" classes. Not being one to give up easily, Ginger's mother then proceeded to voice her request to the principal who finally gave in rather than incur the wrath of this determined parent.

With the help of her mother during the following year Ginger progressed tremendously in her schoolwork. It was then felt by the school counselor that she was functioning at too high a level to be in a special class any longer. Not only had her grades gone from C's and D's to all A's, but upon retesting her it was found that her IQ had jumped from 70 to 110.

This parent was so successful because she challenged her own and other people's assumptions about the abilities of her child. Furthermore, she decided that there was no reason at all why her daughter could not perform at a higher level. When the expectancy level was changed the communications changed, and so did Ginger's behavior.

Another parent's problem was that his six-year-old child was still riding a tricycle while all the other children his age were riding bicycles. The parent felt this was very embarrassing to the child because he would always lag far behind the rest of the group as they played in the neighborhood. The child, however, was quite anxious at the prospect of having to balance on a bigger and scarier bike, and didn't believe he would be successful at it. His parents had put off demanding that he learn to ride, hoping that he would outgrow his fear. They then realized that they also had been afraid their child was not yet capable of riding a bicycle. After examining this belief, they decided that there was no reason why he could not learn to do this at his age and that it would be important to his self-concept that he overcome his fear and be able to play alongside his friends. This decision was, of course, only the beginning. They next had to deal with their child's pleadings that he was afraid and didn't really want to learn, and so on. However, they stuck with their decision, and soon he was enjoying bicycle riding and being able to keep up with his group.

Many parents are not aware of the fact that they have been treating their children as though they were incapable of changing their behavior. It is only by examining the communications of these parents that it becomes clear that they do not really feel that the child can control himself. Therefore, no demands have been made that he do so.

For example, when parents tell children who have soiled themselves or wet the bed that they have "had an accident," this is a clear message that the parent does not believe that the child is responsible for his behavior. An accident is something which nobody controls. Since it is no one's fault, a person cannot be held responsible for making sure it does not happen again. The child is actually being told, "You could not help doing this, and we don't expect you to be able to correct this behavior." This may be an appropriate statement when addressed to a two- or three-year-old, but it is not uncommon to hear a parent of a ten- or eleven-year-old bed wetter state that the child's problem is that he is still having accidents.

Other communications, which imply that the child is unable to control his behavior, are the various labels that parents frequently use in describing their children. "You little thief, liar, brat, show-off, smart aleck," are only a few of the myriad of statements which tell the child that his parents expect that he will continue to act inappropriately. The result of such communications is well-stated in the old saying, "Tell the child often enough that he is bad, and he will soon prove you correct."

Often a quick-witted child will use the labels with which his parents have described his behavior as an excuse for continuing to misbehave. Such was the case when a parent criticized his daughter's behavior by saying, "Why don't you figure out something to do instead of just sitting there, you lazy bum!" The child's response was, "Because I'm a lazy bum!" While this statement may have been made in jest to some extent, generally children do accept their parents' definitions of who they are. Therefore, when a child hears his parents imply that they feel he is incapable of changing his behavior, he very likely will also adopt the same viewpoint.

A METHOD TO HELP PARENTS VIEW THEIR CHILDREN AS CAPABLE OF CHANGING THEIR BEHAVIOR

Step 1 / *Examining and Challenging Parental Ideas*
Parents can avoid communications that imply the child is unable to change his behavior by examining and challenging the ideas they have about why their child is misbehaving in the first place.

If, for instance, a parent believes that his child is misbehaving because "all children do these kinds of things at one time or another," then it is quite obvious this parent believes that since what his child is doing is quite natural, even though somewhat bothersome, there is little that can be done to cause the child to alter his actions. Parents who have such beliefs would never demand that their child cease doing what they felt was "natural" behavior.

One family was having a particularly hard time because of certain beliefs which the parents held about what was "normal" behavior in children.

The Morrises were a large family consisting of two parents and five children, three of whom were boys. The parents were becoming more and more concerned about the sibling rivalry among the three brothers. "This jealousy they have of each other causes them to bicker and fight almost continually," complained Mr. Morris. These "fights" were described as near brawls with furniture and other family valuables often being mutilated in the process.

Mr. and Mrs. Morris had never demanded that this behavior stop, because they genuinely believed that sibling rivalry was a normal thing which all children experience, and that "boys will be boys." The therapist then asked the parents to offer evidence to support their beliefs. They stated that when they were young, both of their families had experienced a great deal of sibling rivalry. "Isn't that the way it is in all families?" Mrs. Morris asked. The therapist responded that while it may be true that nearly all children compete to some extent for their parents' attention and praise, there is certainly no evidence to indicate that they must beat each other up in the process of gaining this attention.

In this case, as with all situations where parents feel that the child is incapable of controlling his behavior, it was necessary to first examine the parents' beliefs about why the child was misbehaving and then to challenge the validity of these ideas by asking the question, "What evidence do you have to support this belief?"

One of the most unusual beliefs about normal behavior that has ever been reported to the authors was held by the mother of a seven-year-old boy. This child, in addition to having set fires in the trash cans at school, had burned down his parents' garage. His mother firmly believed that it was normal for children to play with matches, and that all children surely did this. Again the parent's evidence for this belief was not well-founded, being primarily based on a magazine article that she had read some time ago which talked about the tendency of children to be interested in many things, including matches.

Sometimes parents feel that their child is unable to change his behavior because his problem is caused by past occurrences or other circumstances beyond the child's control. Some of the common beliefs of this type are that the child has a neurological problem, that he is going through a stage, that he has inherited the problem, or that he hasn't had enough attention or love as a child.

NEUROLOGICAL PROBLEM

In the following case, the parents had some evidence to support the belief that their child was minimally brain-damaged. With help from a therapist, they began to see that their convictions were not well-founded.

Theresa just could not sit still for an instant. "We feel this is due to the fact that she fell off a swing when she was three, and this must have caused some sort of brain damage," Theresa's parents explained. Her behavior was a terrible nuisance, they stated, particularly at dinner time when she would fidget and throw food around the table. "Has a doctor confirmed the idea that Theresa suffered some sort of permanent damage in her fall as a child?" the therapist asked. "No," replied the father, "but we've been reading that some neurological problems cannot be detected, and we've also heard that when children can't sit still, it is often related to minimal brain damage." The therapist then asked Theresa's parents to describe the kinds of things they had done to try and get their daughter to behave at the dinner table.

They reported that they had tried the usual assortment of warnings and criticisms without success. To this list they added, without thinking much about it, that every time her behavior became unbearable, they ordered her to a stool in the corner of the kitchen where she was required to sit for up to an hour until the rest of the family had completed their meal. At this time the therapist pointed out that they had been tremendously successful in getting their child to sit still when they had demanded that she do so, but that they had made no such demands at the dinner table.

Even though Theresa's parents believed that she had a neurological problem, when things got to the point where they could not stand her behavior any longer, they demanded the very behavior which they felt she was incapable of, namely that she sit still.

Following this session Theresa was told in no uncertain terms that from now on she was to sit still at the table and not throw food. Her parents were able to insist on this behavior because they had become aware of the fact that their daughter sat still very well when told to do so in terms that were clear an emphatic.

The authors have also treated numerous families in which the child was labeled neurologically impaired and in which there was good medical evidence of the impairment. The critical issue in these cases was to help parents understand the effect of the damage on the child's behavior. Too often these kinds of children are viewed by their parents as incapable of reasonable behavior in any and all areas. This is verified by the child who misbehaves according to his parents' expectations. When the parents are led to question whether the child is really incapable of acting any differently, there is usually no good evidence that the child has to misbehave in these areas. There may be good evidence for limited intellectual achievement or lack of coordination, but rarely is there good evidence that the child has to get into fights, throw tantrums, or other such problem behaviors.

A dramatic example of working with such children was experienced by the senior author during his residency in child psychiatry. Twenty hospitalized medically proven neurologically impaired children with behavioral difficulties were to be taken to the circus. In the hospital they were notorious for their "crazy" behavior. In preparation for the trip the staff had the children practice walking in line, staying together, raising their hands to go to the bathroom, and staying in their seats during a brief performance. The children behaved in their usual bizarre manner on the bus, but the moment they arrived at the circus they formed lines, walked in, and went directly to their seats without any fuss. Other "normal" children were screaming and yelling for balloons and souvenirs, but the hospital group was quiet and orderly. They remained in perfect control during the entire performance, raising their hands to go to the bathroom and laughing and applauding appropriately. After returning to the hospital they resumed their "usual" behavior. At this point one of the staff asked a child why she had behaved so well at the circus and so poorly after returning to the hospital. She replied, "The nurses made us act good at the circus. BUT THAT'S NOT HOW WE ARE SUPPOSED TO ACT AT THE HOSPITAL—WE'RE NOT SUPPOSED TO ACT GOOD AT THE HOSPITAL." When this remark was discussed at the next staff meeting, those in charge of the children were dumbfounded and immediately began reviewing their expectations of these "incapable" children.

PHASES AND STAGES

It is not uncommon to hear parents state that their child's problem is probably a result of a stage he is going through. We have found that this idea is generally little more than wishful thinking. How many people do you know who have suddenly "outgrown" bad habits or self-defeating attitudes? More likely when people change it is a result of great individual determination which has been coupled with pressure from an outside source, such as an employer, spouse, or doctor. Children also rarely "graduate" from behavioral or emotional problems. These difficulties are not outgrown in the same manner as their clothing, toys, or baby furniture. Rather, difficulties tend to increase; because as the world of the child expands to include people and places outside the family, so too do the opportunities for conflicts grow.

Obviously when a parent feels that a child is just in a stage which all children go through, the tendency is to adopt a "wait and see" attitude rather than demanding that the child stop the negative behaviors.

One of the most common stage beliefs which parents and professionals often refer to is the concept of the "terrible twos." This is the year in which everything that is asked of the child is responded to with an immediate no. Often, however, at the same instant that the child is vehemently voicing his opposition to his parents' request, he is already beginning to do as instructed. What this indicates is that the word "no" is for the child a simple means by which he can express his own autonomy or individuality. Certainly this is a difficult time for everyone involved as the child learns the family rules of living. This does not mean, as some have interpreted it, that the child cannot control his behavior or do as he is told. It simply means that at this stage the child may be somewhat more sensitive or resistant to interferences with his behavior.

There are many behaviors which parents generally feel that their children will outgrow. However when these passing phases persist, parents need to reexamine their views as to how long a stage should last.

Martin Leber, like many children, had sucked his thumb beginning at a very young age. It wasn't until he was about seven or eight that his parents became concerned about it. At that time they were not so much worried about the sucking itself, but rather about its possible effects on his teeth. They were also afraid that his classmates and friends might start teasing him. At first they began to try to influence Martin in very subtle ways, such as tying a string around his thumb. This did not work because Martin began sucking on the string as well as his thumb. A war gradually began to escalate between parents and child regarding this problem behavior.

The Lebers had originally seen Martin's behavior as a "stage" which he would eventually grow out of. As it became apparent that this stage might go on indefinitely, Martin's parents then adopted the attitude that Martin was a nervous child and, therefore needed this outlet for his nervousness. (Thus, the parents had switched from a "stage" theory to a "label" which still allowed them to see Martin as incapable of changing his behavior.) Their methods now intensified, but not to the point of demanding that he stop. When Martin was between the ages of ten and fourteen, they tried everything from putting hot pepper on his thumbs to tying his hands at night. However, none of these methods met with any success. At this point, the Lebers came to family therapy.

Martin's parents were shown that they had been very successful in getting their child to do many things that he didn't want to do by insisting that he do these things, but that they had not done so in the case of the thumb-sucking because of their beliefs about his emotional sensitivity. They then modified their position again and decided, because he was already an adolescent by this time, that he was old enough to make the decision of whether he wanted to do this or not. They thought that in this situation their responsibility should be only that of expressing their opinions to their child. As a result, they did not demand that Martin cease his thumb-sucking.

The problem with the Lebers' decision was that it would have been somewhat reasonable had they decided to stop complaining completely about the behavior. However, to continue to criticize a child for his behavior and yet not demand that it stop, is destructive to the child and makes the whole family situation one that is intolerable.

THE PROBLEM HAS BEEN INHERITED

When parents state, whether in criticism or praise, that their child is "just like his father" or "a chip off the old block," the implication is that their child's behavior, attitudes, or skills do not emanate from the child himself, but rather that they are traits he has inherited from his parents or others in the family. The assumption in this case is that if a child can inherit hair and eye color, then it must be that certain behaviors may also be transmitted in this way. Since it is impossible to alter an individual's chromosomes, viewing the child's problem behaviors as being of genetic origin causes parents to see the child as being in no way responsible for what he does and incapable of changing his behaviors, barring a gene transplant. The evidence which parents offer for such beliefs usually relates to the past behavior or attitudes of one of the child's parents, grandparents, uncles, aunts, or sometimes an older sibling. Obviously there is someone in every family, when near and distant relatives are considered, who has engaged in negative behaviors of one sort or another. However there is certainly no evidence to suggest the likelihood of their being a gene which could transmit such tendencies as lying, stealing, and so forth.

Getting parents to challenge their ideas in this regard is not always easy:

Mr. Putnam thought that his child, Chris, had inherited a dislike for school and, at the same time, an appreciation for the outdoors. "It has always been that way on my side of the family," he commented. "What ability we lack in reading books and remembering facts we make up in our knowledge of how to survive in the wild." Chris, as expected, was faring rather poorly in school. The inconsistency in Mr. Putnam's belief about his son's incapability to achieve at school tasks was illustrated by Chris's remarkable memory for names and botanical classifications of literally hundreds of plants and trees in the forest. When Mr. Putnam could not account for this achievement, which was distinctly a school-like task, he was forced to reevaluate his position as to whether Chris had inherited his attitudes toward school, and whether his performance could not be improved. Once these ideas had been called into question, it was easier for Chris's father to see that he had not demanded that Chris do well in school because he believed that his son was not really capable of anything but below-average work. Once these expectations about his son's scholastic ability changed, his communications also changed to an insistance on a higher level of attainment in school.

DEPRIVED IN EARLY CHILDHOOD

The statement "he just didn't get enough love when he was very young," reflects a belief which many parents offer as the reason why they are having difficulties with their children. In this case the parents view their child's misbehavior as an attempt on his part to receive the attention he has been lacking, or as a means to act out his anger at the world which has been cruel to him. It is true that many parents cannot spend as much time as they would like with their young children. Other children have lost one or both of their parents through separation, divorce, or death. Still others may have never known their real parents and spent their early years being shuttled from one foster or group home to another. These children certainly have had a unique and stressful background. However, these experiences in no way predestine a child to develop behavioral or emotional problems. Often difficulties are common with such children because their parents in trying to be sensitive, patient, and flexible are much more tolerant of negative behavior than they would be with children from "normal" backgrounds. It is as if the parents are unknowingly trying to make up for their child's poor start in life. Parents in these cases must ask themselves if allowing the child to get attention or express his hatred of the world by acting in negative ways really helps the child in any way to overcome or change what has happened to him in the past. Would it not be wiser that he be treated and expected to behave like any other child?

But, you may ask, haven't studies shown that children

do have strong emotional reactions to permanent separation from their biological parents even when this occurs in infancy, and don't these emotional reactions inevitably lead to behavioral problems? There is no question that children have stressful reactions to being separated from their parents. However, children have been known to recover from severe emotional traumas and not become behavioral problems when it is demonstrated to them that someone else cares enough to love, take care of, and teach them the rules of living with others.

A psychologist recently interviewed on television indicated that the children coming from Vietnam would have a terribly hard time adjusting to life here due to the vast differences between the two countries, and because of the horrible war experiences these children have undergone. He further stated that these children must have terrible emotional scars that will probably never heal, and that expecting them to become well-adjusted citizens seemed a rather improbable goal. That same day, however, an article appeared in the newspaper which related the story of a girl who, at the age of six, had been found roaming the streets of Saigon "fighting her way through life." She had since been adopted and brought to America where, in spite of her background, she seems to have thrived very well. Not only has she adjusted socially—she even was elected student body president of her junior high school—but she has also maintained a high scholastic average in spite of initial language difficulties. In addition, her parents reported that she has become a happy and responsible member of her family with no evidence of emotional or behavioral problems.

This is not to say that parenting such children is easy. The first few weeks and months may be particularly trying as the child tests the limits of his new environment. Also, children of this type often develop an attitude of not needing or wanting anyone to look after them. If you examine their inner feelings, they might be expressed this way: "Adults are not to be trusted; they will let you down every time. The only person in this world I can trust is me, and I am the one who has to do everything for myself." In spite of these negative attitudes many parents have successfully dealt with children from difficult backgrounds of one sort or another. A large component of this success is that these parents have cared enough to clearly demand appropriate, acceptable behavior from their children.

THE DEVIL MAKES HIM DO IT

The recent popularization of the idea of being "possessed" illustrates an ongoing interest in the idea of being controlled by forces other than one's own mind. In the same vein, not long ago, a group of parents got together and charged that the leaders of a particular religious sect were using mind-control methods to brainwash children into becoming disciples of their causes.

Obviously if it is believed that a child's mind is being controlled from within or without by strange or demonic forces, his parents cannot insist that the child correct his behavior on his own. Magical incantations, prayer, or exorcism become the primary means of returning the child to appropriate behavior. Some parents candidly admit that they believe that their child is possessed. Others may not feel this way consciously, but make reference to such beliefs in their communications about their children's misbehavior. "I'm going to beat the devil out of you"; "Why you little devil, you need some sense knocked into you" are some of the messages that indicate a parent believes that his child's behavior is influenced, if not controlled, by the devil. These communications clearly tell the child that he is not expected to be able to correct his behavior by himself, but that only through dramatic means such as physical punishment can he hope to behave well.

The following case history is an extreme example of a parent feeling that his child's misbehavior was due to the influence of the devil:

> This parent was so certain that his child was possessed that every afternoon he told his son, Kenneth, to relate the things he had done that were bad that day. Then he would take Kenny outside and physically punish him for these misbehaviors. The father, in this case, felt that his child continued to misbehave because he hadn't yet "beat the devil out of him." Meanwhile, Kenny's behavior at school was becoming as violent as his punishment at home. One day on the playground he told a child to wait for him at the bottom of the slide. He then deliberately slid into the child, knocking him down. He than proceeded to jump on and kick the little boy. As if this weren't enough, when his teacher came running over and asked him what had happened, he signaled that she should bend down so that he could whisper something in her ear. He then socked his teacher in the nose. Shortly thereafter Kenny was expelled from school and the principal would not readmit him until the family had been seen by a psychiatrist.

In family therapy the parents related their beliefs that Kenny was possessed by the devil and just could not help behaving as he did. Their solution to this problem was to continue to try to beat the devil out of their child. To do this they felt that they simply needed to "hit him with the right thing in the right place."

This child had heard nearly all his life that he had the devil in him, and that is why he did so many awful things. Therefore, not only did his parents believe this, but Kenny himself felt that he could not control his own behavior. He not only was living up to his parents' expectations, but to his own as well.

There are several other means by which parents view their children as incapable of changing their behavior. One of these is the parental idea that they may be demanding too much of their child, so it would be harmful to ask anything more of him. As one parent put it, "I'm already insisting on quite a few things, and I'm afraid that if I demand anything more, the pressure will be so great on him that he won't be able to do anything at all." The problem in these cases is that these parents do not back off on the things they have been trying unsuccessfully to get their children to do. They simply keep trying to "influence" their children to change their behaviors rather than demanding that these behaviors change. That is, they continue to try to *persuade* their child to change his behavior, but they will not *demand* that he do so. The result is usually that the child continues to behave as he wishes.

A very common reason offered by parents for their child's misbehavior is that he is in with the wrong crowd—that his friends force him to do what he does. This, of course, tells the child very clearly that he is not able to control himself and that he must do what his friends do.

> One parent who was enraged because of his daughter's drug use stated that his daughter was the perfect child, but that she always gets involved with, and is influenced by, the wrong types of people. The daughter insisted that she could control her own behavior and that she took drugs because *she* wanted to, and if she wanted to stop, she could. The parents told her that they did not believe that she could. Obviously, when parents do not believe that the child can stop doing something, they are certainly not going to demand that it stop. In this case the daughter so wanted to prove to her parents that she was an individual human being capable of controlling her own behavior that she stopped using drugs completely.

Adolescents, in particular, rebel against the idea that they have to do things because their friends do them. Parents would do well to remember that even though a child's peer group is important, that doesn't mean the child is incapable of saying to his friends, "This is something I do not do." If his friends do not accept that, then the child is also capable of choosing friends who are more sympathetic to his position.

As we have stated throughout this chapter, when parents feel that their child is incapable of controlling his behavior, the child, too, comes to accept and believe this view of himself. Often when parents start demanding that he change his behavior, he will not accept the idea that this is something which he can really accomplish. The reason for this is that he has probably heard, day after day, communications such as those enumerated in this chapter which imply that he is neither responsible for, nor able to change, his behavior.

It is up to the parents in these cases to erode the child's self-doubt. This can be accomplished through the same process by which the parents altered their own conceptions of their child's capabilities. That is, by demonstrating that there really was no evidence for the parents' beliefs, and that now since there is no reason to expect that the child cannot change his behavior, that behavior will be changed. When the child becomes aware of the fact that his parents think differently about him, this enables him to think differently about himself The often-quoted precept, "I am what I think others think I am," clearly illustrates the effect that people's opinions of us have on our self-image. To the child the most significant and influential "others" are, of course, his parents.

The following case demonstrates the procedure that parents may use to inform their child that they no longer see him as incapable of changing his behavior:

> Annie's parents heard a lecture on "How to Get Your Children to Do What You Want Them to Do." They had come because Annie, who was ten, was still wetting the bed. Her parents felt that this was due to Annie's being hyperactive, and also because she ran around so much all day long that she was incredibly worn out by nightfall and, therefore, slept so deeply that she could not wake up to go to the bathroom. After the lecture they related to the guest

speaker their ideas about why Annie was still wetting the bed.

This "story" seemed logical and foolproof at first hearing. However no testing had been done to determine that Annie was hyperactive, and, furthermore, she had often been dry when the parents went on vacation. On these occasions the parents made it very clear that Annie was to "not wet the sheets, because it would be difficult to clean them, since there wasn't any washing machine nearby like at home." These facts were then pointed out to the parents who then decided that Annie definitely was capable of changing her behavior. However, unlike regular family therapy where the child is present to hear these ideas challenged, the parents then had to return home and communicate their new insight to their child. They simply said to her, "You know, we've been thinking about your bed-wetting, and we remembered that the last time we went away on vacation you were dry every night. Since you are able to do this some of the time, there is no reason why you cannot do it all of the time. We have been wrong in telling you that this is something that is very hard for you. We no longer think it is so hard for you after all, because you have shown us that this is not the case. So under no circumstances are you to wet the bed ever again."

This was a behavior which had gone on for as long as this child had been alive, yet when her parents communicated their confidence in her by insisting that she stay dry, the child was able to correct the behavior within one week.

CHALLENGING PARENTAL IDEAS ABOUT THEIR CHILDREN'S MISBEHAVIOR

Reasons for Misbehaving	Questions to Challenge the Validity of These Reasons
1. *All children engage in the behavior* Fight with their siblings Play with matches "Boys will be boys"	Are there no exceptions? Is the belief based solely on the personal experiences of the parents?
2. *Phases and Stages* Terrible twos Adolescent rebellion	How long will I wait for the child to outgrow the stage? Even if this is a stage, what evidence is there that the child cannot perform a particular behavior in spite of this?
3. *The problem has been inherited* The bad seed, black sheep, child with bad blood, etc.	What evidence is there that genes can transmit negative behavior? Under what circumstances has the child performed desired behavior in spite of his inheritance?
4. *Deprived in early childhood* The one parent child	How will allowing the child to do as he wishes in all respects make up for his deprivations?

Continued

The foster child The adopted child The rejected child	How does being deprived cause a child to do specific things like steal, lie, etc.?
5. *Possession* The devil made him do it	What evidence is there for this belief?

In Chapter 3 it was shown that when parents are not sure what their child can do, they also do not insist that the child's behavior change. The following common excuses or beliefs were examined: "All children behave this way"; "The child has a neurological problem"; "It's just a phase"; "The problem has been inherited"; and "He was deprived as a small child." In avoiding this third pitfall, parents must first become aware of the beliefs they have about the child's problem, and then challenge these ideas to see if there is valid evidence to substantiate these beliefs. If the ideas are found to be lacking in proof, then the parents must not only redirect their own attitudes about what their child is capable of, but they must also convince the child that the parents' previous ideas have been faulty. After this the parents can successfully alter their child's behavior by demanding that the behavior be changed.

Up to this point we have discussed how parents can avoid the three parental pitfalls. In the section that follows, a case history will be presented which shows how the parental pitfalls are related to one another. In addition, by using the family intervention work sheet (appearing later in the book), the reader is given a step-by-step method to correct any problem behaviors his child may presently be having.

PART TWO

CHANGING PROBLEM BEHAVIORS

4

WHERE TO START WITH YOUR CHILD
Intervention/Prevention

Step 1 / *Existing Problem Behaviors*
The starting point for changing your child's problem behaviors is to draw up a list of those behaviors, putting the most important one at the top. These are your "goals" and they must be very specific. Avoid general terms like "hostility," "depression," "stubborn," and so on. Make sure that you focus on the problem directly, avoiding goals like getting your child to "try" to sit still or to "learn" to do his homework. The direct goals in these cases would be that your child sit still or do his homework.

Enter your list of goals on the family intervention work sheet. Go over this list with your husband, wife, or anyone else who is presently in a parental relationship with your child. It is important that parents agree to back one another on a goal or decide that the goal is not really worth the effort.

In the sample intervention work sheet both parents agreed that the most important goal they had for their eight-year-old child was that he not ride his bicycle in the street.

Using this goal as their starting place for intervention, they went on to the next step.

Step 2 / *Reasons Why Parents Feel Their Child Is Misbehaving*

When you have decided on the most important behavior that you wish to change, the next step is to write down the ideas you have as to why your child is misbehaving. Then you must challenge these ideas to see whether they are really valid. In the case of the child who rode his bicycle in the street, his parents felt he did this because all the other children did it. This is a way of saying that he cannot stop himself from riding in the street; that he is incapable of behaving any differently. It gives the child a valid excuse for his behavior. Before his parents could do anything about changing his riding habit, they first had to challenge the notion that their child must do something because "all the other children do it." In the course of thinking about this matter, they realized that there were many other things that "all the children" did which their child did not do, things such as eating certain foods which they did not allow their child to eat. They found that even though the other children were allowed to eat these foods, their child would not, even when unsupervised. Once they realized that he was capable of acting independently of his friends they saw that there was no valid reason for their child to ride his bicycle in the street. They were then ready for the next step in changing this behavior.

It is crucial therefore to be aware of any "incapabilities of changing" which you may have regarding your child's misbehavior. Do you see your child as a "little devil," or a "chip off the old block"? Do you label him a "shy" child, or do you think of his problem as just being a "stage" he's going through? All of these beliefs are excuses for the child's behavior and must be challenged before moving on to the next step.

Step 3 / *Unsuccessful Approaches to Stop Misbehavior*
Write down all the things you have said or done to try and get your child to change. It is important that you note the exact words as stated to your child. In the sample case, the parents had tried taking the bicycle away for a day or two, reasoning with the child that he could get hurt if he were to ride in the street, and had spanked him on occasion—all to no avail.

As you know by now, none of these approaches is a demand that the child stop riding in the street.

Step 4 / *Examples of Successes*
Enter one or two examples of times when you got your child to do something even though he did not want to do it. This is a very important step. Again, write down exactly what you said or did. Every parent can think of such an occasion. How do you get your child to go to school, for instance, when he doesn't want to? One mother complained that she could not get her child to do anything at all. However, it was discovered that one time her child was playing "superman" on the roof of the house and was about to fly off to nab a crook when she saw him and yelled "climb down off that roof now and don't ever go up there again." This child knew that she meant what she said and his roof-climbing days were over.

We have frequently found that one area in which parents are quite successful is in punishing their children. Although that sounds a little peculiar, punishing children often involves making demands. To illustrate, take the case of Mrs. Lewis:

She complained that her daughter could not be made to do anything she didn't want to do. She almost had to physically drag her to the family therapy session. "What do you say or do to your daughter when you've really had it with her?" asked the therapist. "I pretty much do the same thing every time," Mrs. Lewis replied. "I tell her OK, that's it, now you just get in your room and stay there until I tell you to come out. She knows better than to even poke her head out of the bedroom door." "I see," stated the therapist. "You are a very successful parent after all. When you tell your daughter to go to her room and she stays there and will not even poke her head out of the door, you have 'demanded' that she obey you. So you are 'successful' in getting your child to do what you want when you really mean it."

Use *your* success examples as proof that you can get your child to do what you want.

Step 5 / *Putting It All Together*
Now you have a clear idea of what you want your child to do (Step 1), and you see your child as capable of doing this (Step 2). You also have reviewed the approaches that have not worked in getting him to change (Step 3), and the approach that has worked with other behaviors (Step 4). Now compare your communications about the problem behavior with the communications when you are successful. Nearly always the difference is that effective communications are *demands* whereas the unsuccessful communications are not. In addition, the reason parents do not use demands is because they are not quite sure that their child is

capable of changing his behavior. Now that you see your child as being able to do the behavior you wish, there is no reason for you not to demand that he change.

It must be remembered that demands are more than words alone. To mean what you say may involve getting angry, being firm, changing your body posture or tone of voice—all the ingredients that are present when your child knows that you really mean what you're saying.

SAMPLE INTERVENTION WORK SHEET

Step 1 / *Listing the Problem Behaviors*

>*Most Important Goal*
>Getting child to stop riding bike in street.

>*Other Goals*
>Stop hitting sister
>Clean room once a week
>Be home by four o'clock after school

Step 2 / *Reasons Why Parents Feel Their Child Is Misbehaving*

>Parents felt their child rode his bike in the street because all of the other children did so. They challenged this idea and realized that he did not do everything that the other children did, e.g. would not eat "junk" foods because parents clearly forbid it.

Step 3 / *Unsuccessful Approaches to Stop Misbehavior*

>Parents have tried taking the bicycle away for a day or two, reasoning with the child that he could get

hurt if he rode in the street, and had spanked him occasionally.

Step 4 / *Examples of Successes*

Parents had been very successful at getting child to not eat "junk" food. They very firmly told him, "You are not to eat candy or soda pop except once a month at a special meal in our home." He had complained for a while about this but soon realized that his parents meant what they said and would not back down.

Step 5 / *Putting It All Together*

These parents now have a clear idea of what they want their child to do (not ride in the street); they now see that they used to view their child as incapable of changing, but have now challenged that belief (all the kids do it); they know which approaches do not work in changing a behavior (spanking, reasoning, punishments); and they know which approaches do work (clear and firm demands).

There is now no reason for them not to demand that the child no longer ride his bicycle in the street. (This family did exactly that in a very direct and meaningful way and reported shortly thereafter that this was no longer a problem.)

After changing this behavior, these parents were ready to proceed to the next goal on their list on the Family Intervention Work Sheet—to stop hitting his sister. (If you have a particularly long list, what typically happens is that after you have successfully changed two or three of the important behaviors, the child realizes that misbehaviors will not be tolerated and he begins to change on his own at that point.)

FAMILY INTERVENTION WORK SHEET

Step 1 / *Listing the Problem Behaviors*
  Most Important Goal

  Other Goals

Step 2 / *Reasons Why Parents Feel Their Child Is Misbehaving*
  A. Reasons

  B. Challenge Validity of Reasons

Step 3 / *Unsuccessful Approaches to Stop Misbehavior*

Step 4 / *Examples of Successes*
  (Times when parents were successful at getting child to do something he did not want to do)

Step 5 / *Putting It All Together*

PREVENTION

Throughout the book we have been discussing a means by which parents can correct their children's misbehaviors. To prevent problem behaviors from developing in the first place IT IS IMPERATIVE THAT PARENTS ADJUST THEIR COMMUNICATIONS TO FIT THE TYPE OF CHILD THEY HAVE. It may seem strange to learn that different children require a different approach in getting them to do what you want, but scientific research has shown that there are significant differences in children and that these differences are even detectable in the fetus as well as in the infant in the first hours after birth. As one parent put it, "I can't believe how different my children are when it comes to getting them to do things. For instance, if I notice that the trash is piling up and I say to Alan, 'It sure is getting messy in here,' he takes it out without a word. If I say something like that to Keith, it goes in one ear and out the other. To get him to take out the trash I literally have to put the wastepaper basket in his hand and point him to the door."

It certainly would be simpler and more convenient if all children were the same. The fact is, as any parent who has had more than one child can testify, no two children are alike. Some respond without question or resistance to almost anything their parents request. Children of this type may not enjoy doing what has been asked of them, but they do not usually challenge their parents' decisions about what it is they are to do. With such children various types of communications may work. You may rarely have to "demand" anything of such a child. In fact, to suddenly demand things of a child who normally does what he is told merely by requesting it, would be inappropriate. At the other extreme there is the child who, no matter what his parents want done, procrastinates, ignores, or argues about his parents' directions. To this child every parental wish is a battleground and demands will often be the only language that he understands. The "difficult" child requires more in every way from his parents than the "easy" child. He needs more supervision, more reminding, more structure, and infinitely more patience. However, these children can be as wonderfully enjoyable as any child when the "rules of living" are clearly spelled out. The most successful way to do this is to communicate parental expectations in clear demands and to follow through on them. Your child may not thank you immediately (if ever) for your dedication, but the long-range benefits will prove to be worth the effort.

In addition to knowing what type of child you have (one that is difficult or relatively easy to discipline), it can also be helpful to understand the type of child *you* were. Parents often determine how to raise their children based on the type of childhood they have had. For example, in family therapy we frequently see parents who as children had been treated very strictly and who have taken the opposite extreme with their own children. They wish to raise a free spirit, a child unfettered by discipline and "have-to's." It is a noble goal. Unfortunately, however, it will not work with all children. As we stated before, some children, regardless of their parents' philosophy, need limits on their behavior which are clearly spelled out, as well as a great deal of supervision. Such was the case with Alan, aged five.

Alan was virtually a terror at the nursery school he attended. The teachers were at their wits' end with him. He would kick the other children with his cowboy boots, had taken a scissors and injured another child with it, and was never where he was supposed to be. When his parents came for counseling, they at first stated that they had no problems with him at home and were very surprised to hear of his behavior at school. As the session progressed it became clear that they too had been having a difficult time with him, but it was hard for them to admit this because they were very sensitive about the fact that they had been trying a new and more liberal way to raise children and they did not want to admit defeat. They felt they had been raised very strictly and they had wanted their child to be a sweet and free, loving and gentle spirit. He was certainly none of those things by the time he was seen in family therapy. His parents very quickly realized they had been reacting too strongly to their own upbringing. One stated finally, "I guess not everything my mother did was wrong."

Up to this point they had been making up a variety of excuses for Alan's behavior: he kicked the children with his boots because he loved his boots so much he could not keep them off the other boys and girls; he let the air out of his father's tires because he was very curious; he smeared cosmetics all over his mother's mirror because he was creative and artistic. They began to doubt some of the reasons

they had been offering for his behavior and instead
realized that he did these things essentially because
he was in total control of them. The situation was
not good for him or for their sanity.

It would be easier if we could have predetermined
philosophies as parents and then just put them into
action, but as this case has shown, parents must continually look at their "real" child, not the child they have
made up in their heads.

The following is another example of how a parent's
childhood influenced her own attitude toward the
parental role.

Paula was having difficulty in managing her six-year-
old. He was very much in control of her. He was constantly testing her to see what he could get away
with and it really was not much of a contest. He usually won without too much effort. In discussing
this fact with her, she began to reflect on her relationship with her own parents. It had been a very
difficult one, she stated, and now at the age of
twenty-nine she felt like she was totally disinterested
in them and quite detached emotionally as well as
geographically from their lives. She saw this as very
unfortunate and was dead set against its happening
between her and her son. Unfortunately, she thought
that by being overly tolerant of his desires and behaviors she would raise a child who would be very
appreciative and thankful for all of the indulgences
throughout the years. Nothing could have been further from the truth. Although he pretty much got
his way in everything, he never seemed satisfied or

appreciative about anything. No matter what she did to try to please him, nothing was ever enough. He would always want more. What little she did demand of him was responded to with tremendous outbursts of temper and complaints. Surely her scheme for raising a child who would be close to his parent was not going as planned.

What was going wrong in this relationship to make this child so apparently ungrateful? The authors have observed many such children who were getting everything they wanted yet somehow seemed unhappy. We believe the reason for this is that children do not feel comfortable with more power than they are capable of handling. They do not always act as if this is so. They often complain when forced to comply with those who are more "powerful" than they. But the fact is that deep inside they would rather leave the "driving" to the person who has more experience. Of course children will not turn down the chance to exercise control over their parents, because power is very attractive to them. (This is true of adults as well. Think of the people who take on promotions above their abilities. The prestige and power associated with the new job has tremendous appeal. However, in many cases, the person experiences tremendous anxiety and often is less happy than in his previous role.) Such is the case with children. On the one hand, to be able to manipulate one's parents is very exciting. However, children who wield too much power experience anxiety because they know they are over their heads and really wish that their parents would take over at the wheel.

The *way* in which our own parents got us to do what

they wanted can also strongly affect the way in which we direct our children.

The Carleys came to family therapy with their five-year-old, Richard, who was a toilet-training problem. The therapist went through the usual steps of showing the parents how they had not been demanding that the child do as they wish, but rather had been threatening the child, labeling his behavior as immature, and spanking him on occasion. To this Richard's father replied that when he was a child he would never do anything his parents wished unless there was a threat of punishment involved. Because of this experience, it was apparent that he believed the only way he could get Richard to do something he didn't want to do was to frighten him into doing it. This had worked with some behaviors but it had not worked with the toilet training.

It was the therapist's task to convince Mr. Carley that demands were a more effective way of getting children to do things. The problem was that Richard's father had never used demands with his son, so it was impossible to find an example of his being successful in this way. However Richard's mother had been effective in getting her son to clean up his room even though he hated doing so. "What is it that you say or do to get him to obey you in cleaning the room?" the therapist asked. "It's not easy," she replied. "At first I had to stand over him the whole time and tell him over and over to clean it up. Now he knows I mean it and does it with only a little complaining." The therapist then pointed out to Mr. Carley how successful his wife had been without using threats. After discussing this for a while, the therapist decided to see if Richard's father really understood and was prepared now to use demands instead of threats with the toilet-training problem:

Therapist: I'm wondering what you are going to say to Richard now about his using the toilet?

Mr. Carley: I'm going to tell him that the next time he soils himself, I'll give him a spanking he won't forget.

Even after an hour of discussing the difference between demands and threats, this father would still not make a demand of his child. Instead he gave the child a choice of either using the toilet or getting a spanking. The problem with Mr. Carley was that his own childhood experiences made it very difficult for him to understand a different way of handling children even though his wife had several examples of alternative methods. Gradually over the next few weeks, this father overcame his ideas about parenting and became more effective in making clear demands.

In addition to reflecting on the type of childhood you have had, it would be helpful to jot down any problem behaviors which were "battlegrounds" between you and your parents. Often the areas that were battlegrounds for you as a child become problem behaviors for your own children. There are many examples of this occurring with such behaviors as bed-wetting, stealing, getting in fights at school, keeping a messy bedroom, and so on.

such as "priorities"
doing it my own sweet time.

Behaviors like this get passed on from generation to generation because the parents start to feel that somehow the child has "inherited" a tendency to behave in this way.

> Jan brought her daughter in for family therapy because she just could not stand the mess her daughter made in the bathroom and bedroom.

> *Jan:* I just can't take it any longer. I can't get in her bedroom because the door gets caught in her clothes which are all over the floor. I'm so embarrassed for her that I go and clean her mess up so that she can have friends over. I tried forbidding her to have guests over but she would rather sit in there, mess and all, than to clean it up. I guess she's just like me. My mom tried and tried to get me to clean my room and I wouldn't either; it must run in the family.

As we stated in Chapter 3, when parents believe that their child has inherited a behavioral pattern, they see the child as incapable of acting any other way and therefore do not demand that he change.

5

QUESTIONS
AND ANSWERS

Q. Isn't this a rather unfeeling and authoritarian
way to raise children?

A Only if it is looked upon as a total child-rearing
approach. It is not. Many sensitive and well-written
books delineate the growing child's needs in areas
other than the ones explored in this book. There
is no conflict, however, between attending to these
other needs and also attending to a child's need for
clear demands. For instance, there is no reason why
a parent cannot be nurturing and understanding
and at the same time very clear about what the child
is and is not allowed to do; there is no reason why
parents cannot give their children plenty of choices
and freedom and yet hold steadfastly to those standards which they feel are vitally important.

Throughout the book we have taken the position that
before making a demand, parents should be really sure
of the importance of that behavior. They should ask
themselves, "Is this worth the effort that making a
demand requires?" Parents should make demands only
when the answer is an unequivocal yes.

The real danger to children is not in making too many
demands of them but rather hassling over their behaviors
while not demanding that they cease. This hassling

109

inevitably leads to an increasingly destructive authority battle in the parent-child relationship. Consider a parent who tells his child: "If you don't get all *B*'s this semester, then you will not be able to participate in any Boy Scout activities." At the end of the semester the child gets less than a *B* average and the parent then states: "What's wrong with you? I told you to get *B*'s. You never do what you're told, do you?" It is this type of parent who is being unjustifiably cruel because he did not tell his child to get *B*'s. He gave him a choice between *B*'s and Boy Scouts—a choice he didn't really mean to give.

The best argument for demands is the response of the children themselves when their parents become more authoritative. It has been our repeated experience that children who are out of control are extremely anxious and unhappy. However, once their parents start setting limits effectively, these children not only behave better, they actually feel better.

A clear example of this phenomenon is demonstrated in the following case:

> A ten-year-old boy was brought in by his parents because of many severe behavioral problems. It immediately became clear that the boy was in control of his parents when he told them, "Shut up, I'll tell the story to the doctor and answer all the questions myself." At the end of the first session his parents saw their dilemma and chose to correct the situation by clearly assuming the parental role in the family. In the second session they reported that not only had the child's behavior markedly improved, but for the first time in his life "he was

being physically affectionate with his parents and making friends with other children."

There is a tendency to view "demanding" things of a child as reminiscent of the earlier more harsh ways of raising children. Images come to mind of cold, aloof parents who were very strict and who never explained the reasons why you had to do things. There is no reason why parents cannot combine a firm set of values with the other qualities of parenting which are important also. Much has been written about these other qualities, so little needs to be said here about them. In fact, there is a danger in emphasizing these other characteristics of the parental role because sometimes in doing so parents lose sight of what is most fundamental—establishing very clearly who is in the leadership role in the family. Some parents, having learned of the sensitive nature of the child's mind during the first several years, have been afraid to be too firm about anything lest they "cripple" their child emotionally for the rest of his life. Keeping in mind that children have a great need for parents who are sure of their own values and willing to back them up, it is then safe to emphasize the child's obvious need to feel that he is a worthwhile and lovable person. We are all familiar with people who spend a great part of their adult lives trying to win the approval and favor of others so that they can feel good about themselves. Most often this is the result of their not having developed a sense of their own worth as children within the family structure. Certainly other influences can make a child question his self-worth besides his parents' response to him. However, armed with sufficient acceptance and appreciation from home, a child is greatly fortified against the onslaught of competition he will find in the unprotected environments outside his family.

It is important that the acceptance and appreciation he experiences from his family are not solely based on what he does or doesn't do, but rather are based on the fact that he just *is*. He must develop a sense of: "I am good and worthwhile merely because I exist. I do not have to prove my goodness."

The task of instilling such a degree of self-acceptance is not an easy one. Combining this with the need to also limit the child's behavior in many areas makes parenting the most difficult of all occupations. Realizing this, it is important to not expect perfection from yourself as a parent while at the same time holding onto your dream of a full and beautiful life for your children.

Q. What about when there is only one parent, particularly the single mother? Does demanding still work?

A. Often women who are raising their children alone believe that they are not capable of maintaining the authority role in the family. They do not feel confident that they can get their children to do what they want through direct and firm demands. The truth is that many women have been tremendously successful in raising a family of either sex totally on their own. One of the authors is familiar with a single mother of nine children who is a very effective parent, setting limits well and maintaining a positive relationship with her children.

There is no question that the job of raising a child by oneself makes parenting more difficult. It is certainly helpful to have someone on whom you can depend to back you up, to lend support, to assist with the many responsibilities of being a parent. However as far as being capable of and potent enough to be a successful parent, one person is all that is necessary.

Involved with the issue of raising children alone is the child's attitude toward the loss of one parent, whether partially as in the case of a divorce or permanently if the parent has died. As mentioned previously, children respond to stress differently from adults. An adult can talk out his anxieties. He can use reasoning to help him understand and accept life's realities. A child is somewhat incapable of this, and his reasoning may lead him to believe that since one parent has left him there is a possibility that he will lose his other parent also. The child may deal with his anxiety through increased misbehavior. It is as if through such misbehavior he is questioning whether his remaining parent will still be a parent to him. During this trying period it is important for the parent to reemphasize the fact that the child can depend on continued guidance and nurturance from his remaining parent.

Q. Aren't the concepts you have been talking about similar to the behavior modification approach?

A. Only in the sense that in this book, as with behavior modification, the child's specific behaviors are focused upon. At that point, though, the similarity ends. Behavior modification is based on the principles of learning theory which state that behaviors that are rewarded will tend to be repeated while those that are punished will disappear. For example, a parent might reward a child with a lollipop everytime he used the toilet appropriately. It is the position of this book that there is nothing wrong with rewards per se. What is crucial is the way in which they are presented. If the parent says, "If you use the toilet you will get a lollipop," the choice about the matter is left with the child. He may or may not do it, depending on how much he likes lollipops. Many times no matter what the reward, the child will not change his behavior. If, however, the parent says, "When you use the toilet you will get a lollipop," it is clear that the child has to do this but that in addition there will be a reward for the behavior.

Another problem with the use of rewards was demonstrated by a parent whose children would not do anything without getting something for their efforts. This parent had been brainwashed into thinking that she had no power as a parent except that of a "goodie" dispenser. She was actually hesitant to ask things of her children because she was afraid that it might cost her. The lesson of this example is that rewards can make chores more pleasant for children, but they do not replace parental authority.

A final difficulty with behavior modification is in using punishments to deter behavior. We have given many examples throughout the book of punishments of every kind which parents have levied against their children. If, as learning theory states, "punishment decreases behavior," why doesn't it work? Learning theorists will state that when punishments don't work it is because you are really rewarding the child with the *attention* that a spanking or a scolding gives him, and that the parent needs to *ignore* the behavior instead. This may seem plausible with certain behaviors, such as using profanity, but can you seriously imagine a parent ignoring a child's setting fires, stealing cars, or running away from home?

It is much simpler and much more direct for parents to know *one way* to get their children to do or not to do things, which they can then apply to every possible situation. We feel this is what this book offers. Behavior modification, on the other hand, requires a different approach with every situation and continual readjustments if the rewards or punishments do not work.

Q. I can understand demanding things of younger children, but what about the adolescent? Doesn't he need to learn to make decisions and accept the consequences of those choices?

A. In dealing with teenagers, parents have to be careful to evaluate what behaviors of their child are crucial and unmodifiable, and which are not all that important. There are two reasons for doing this. One is that there is a price one has to pay for making demands. Parents must be willing to pay this price in order for the child to know that his parents really mean what they say. This involves following through on the demands, not backing down, and stating the demand in firm and unequivocal terms. All this is really quite a hassle and, to preserve their sanity, parents must limit this hassling to those behaviors for which there is no alternative. The second reason for limiting demands is to avoid a problem which causes great resentment in the adolescent—feeling that there is no area of his life which is *his* area to decide, that even in the smallest of decisions he must consult, that no matter what it is his parents have an opinion which is the correct one, and to do otherwise is to be immature and inexperienced. To avoid this situation, parents must allow the child some latitude by allowing decisions and freedom within those areas of behavior that are merely a matter of preference and not really of prime importance. The specific behaviors which fall into each category will differ from family to family. Some parents will put more value on schooling, friends, or appearance than other parents. No matter where the emphasis is placed, there must be an area which belongs solely to the child, and in this area he should be granted total autonomy. It is with these behaviors that the adolescent learns to make decisions.

Q. What about parents who demand too much of their children?

A. Often what appear to be excessive demands or expectations of a child turn out to be confusion about what the parents really want the child to do. When parents can be helped to clarify exactly what behaviors they wish, it is extremely rare that they will demand a behavior which is unrealistic in terms of the child's capabilities.

In the following case the parents seemed to be unrealistic in their demands; however the real problem was one of clarifying their fears and anxieties about what they throught their child might do.

The Simpsons had decided to restrict their seventeen-year-old son to the house because he had gotten into trouble with drug use at school. They intended to keep him restricted in this manner until he was eighteen. The parents were afraid that this was unfair and excessive control, but they didn't know what else to do. When they were shown that they could deal with the drug use problem directly, they then demanded that he not use them while living at home. Thus, by focusing on the real problem, they changed their demand from one that seemed unreasonable to one that was more appropriate.

Q. I understand how parents can make demands of a child in situations where the parents are around to supervise, but what about when the child is out of sight, for example in school.

A. Parents still have power and influence over their children regardless of where that child may be. Many people are still doing exactly what they had been told to do as a child years after they left home. In the case of a child at school, he will do what he is told even in that situation if the communications are very clear, e.g. "Do not get out of your seat without permission," and if the parent cares enough to find out what the child is doing in class, communications can be adjusted to the situation. We have used this same approach effectively in getting parents to understand that they are even more powerful, if they choose to be, than the child's peer group. Again, if parents communicate precisely what their child can and cannot do, the child is capable of telling his friends, "I cannot go along with you on this." He can also be helped to understand that if his friends cannot accept his being different, then it might be better for him to consider making other acquaintances.

Q. Can the ideas presented in this book be applied in settings outside the home environment?
A. Yes, the ideas and techniques outlined in this book have many other applications beyond the typical family. The authors have experienced great success with this approach in such diverse areas as schools, juvenile justice (probation), child abuse, and foster care.

Schools

The most powerful and influential force in an elementary school student's life is not the teacher, but his or her parents. Recognizing this, teachers using the techniques discussed in this book have been successful in encouraging parents to take an active role in their child's education. This has resulted in better achievement and fewer behavioral problems in the classroom. The teachers have cooperated with clear, precise observations and reports to the parents, allowing the parents then to communicate their demands to their children.

Juvenile Justice (Probation)

The senior author has functioned as a consultant and trainer to the Probation Department for over five years. Several diversion/alternative programs have been developed using the techniques set forth in this book with excellent success. The emphasis has been on helping parents clarify their problems with their children and reinforcing the parents' capabilities of controlling the aberrant behavior. Another use has been in detention facilities, where staff members have been trained to communicate clearly and effectively with their wards, with significant decrease in behavioral problems and runaways.

Child Abuse

This approach has been extremely popular with professionals working with child-abusing families. They help parents clarify which behaviors are really important for their children and which behaviors really do not matter. The parents can then be successful in demanding the important behaviors and avoid involvement in the insignificant ones. This frees the parent and the child from the constant battle and harangue. When this is accomplished, the parent no longer feels the hopelessness, helplessness, and frustration which are the hallmarks of child abuse, and the abuse stops.

Foster Care

Taking responsibility for someone else's children is an occupation fraught with many problems. The ideas expressed in this book have been taught to a pilot project group of foster parents and their social workers. The results have been very encouraging with decreased behavioral problems in the children and increased success and satisfaction in the foster parents. An extension of this has involved natural parents working with foster parents for return of the children to their natural families.

BIBLIOGRAPHY
BEYOND GETTING YOUR CHILDREN TO DO WHAT YOU WANT

At the outset of this book, we stated that there is a great deal more to parenting than getting children to do what you want them to do. To establish a secure leadership role is fundamental, but it is only the starting point for a full and exciting parent-child relationship. Thankfully, there are many valuable books on aspects of parenting which we have not touched upon in our treatise on problem behaviors. Many of these books are listed and described on the following pages. Though by no means an exhaustive reference guide, the books do represent the spectrum of issues related to the growth of children and their parents.

1. HELPING PARENTS UNDERSTAND THEMSELVES

James, Muriel, and Dorothy Jongeward, *Born to Win.* Reading, Mass.: Addison-Wesley Pub. Co., 1971.
> Can greatly increase a parent's self-awareness and help the individual better understand what he wants to change in his relationship with his children.

Rogers, Carl, *On Becoming a Person.* Boston: Houghton-Mifflin Co., 1961.

Sheehy, Gail, *Passages.* New York: E. P. Dutton, 1976.
> An important work which delineates the stages of adult growth and development.

BIBLIOGRAPHY

2. OPENING UP COMMUNICATION BETWEEN PARENTS AND CHILDREN

Bessell, Harold and Waldo Palomares, *Human Development Program.* El Cajon, Calif.: Human Development Training Institute, 1972.
> Activities for the family as a whole which can facilitate honest and open communication.

→ Ginott, Haim, *Between Parent and Child.* New York: Macmillan Co., 1969.
> Helpful book for understanding how to talk and listen to children. Prepares parents for typical children's questions.

→ Gordon, Thomas, *Parent Effectiveness Training.* New York: Wyden, 1970.
> A good book on how to listen to children. Do not recommend chapter on changing problem behaviors, as it may be inappropriate for "difficult" children.

3. UNDERSTANDING THE COGNITIVE AND PHYSICAL GROWTH OF THE CHILD

Gesell, Arnold and Frances Ilg, *The Child from Five to Ten.* New York: Harper, 1946; *Youth* (10-16). New York: Harper & Row, Pub., 1956.
> These books provide data on normal developmental milestones regarding children's physical growth and capabilities. You should use them as general guides only and not over-react if your child is a few months ahead of or behind the norms.

Hymes, James L., *The Child Under Six.* Englewood Cliffs, New Jersey: Prentice-Hall, 1963.
> A sensitive and exciting book which shows how the

groundwork for later personality development is laid in the first six years.

Spock, Benjamin, *Baby and Child Care.* New York: Pocket Books, Inc., 1957.

A classic; contains much valuable information for new parents about everyday occurrences in the life of the developing child and how they should be responded to.

Stone, Joseph, and Joseph Church, *Childhood and Adolescence.* New York: Random House, 1957.

Typically used as a textbook but not difficult to read. A good overview of physical, emotional, language and cognitive development.

4. CHILDREN WITH DEVELOPMENTAL PROBLEMS

Feingold, Bernard, *Why Your Child Is Hyperactive.* New York: Random House, 1974.

"Children With Special Handicaps," Supterintendent of Documents, Department of Health, Education and Welfare, U.S. Government Printing Office. Washington 25, D.C.

Kephart, Newell, *The Slow Learner in the Classroom.* Columbus, Ohio: Charles Merrill, 1960.

Classic in the field of understanding children with learning disabilities.

5. KEEPING UP ON CURRENT INFORMATION REGARDING CHILDREN AND PARENT-CHILD RELATIONS

Pamphlets and Journals:

"Young Children," Published by the National Association for the Education of Young Children, 1834 Connecticut Ave. N.W. Washington, D.C.

BIBLIOGRAPHY

"Coming of Age," Problems of Teen-agers; Saving Your Marriage, How to Tell Your Child About Sex. Public Affairs Pamphlets, 22 E. 38th Street, New York 16, New York.

6. BOOKS TO HELP CHILDREN UNDERSTAND THEMSELVES AND THEIR EMOTIONS

Gardner, Richard, *Boys & Girls Book About Divorce*. Bantam Books, 1971.

Hall, Marie, *Play with Me*. New York: Viking Press, 1968.

Heidi, Florence, *Some Things Are Scary*. New York: Star Pub. Co., 1971.

Hoban, Russel, *Best Friends for Frances*. New York: Harper and Row, 1969.

Helps children understand their relations with siblings.

Kraus, Robert, *Leo the Late Bloomer*. New York: Young Readers, Inc., 1973.

Helps children appreciate that they are continually developing skills and will soon be able to do things which are out of their reach at present.

Zolotow, Charlotte, *William's Doll*. New York: Harper and Row, 1972.

The Menninger Foundation, through Western Publishing Co., Racine, Wisc. offers a variety of books which, in story form, help children understand and accept emotions such as jealousy, anger, and fear.